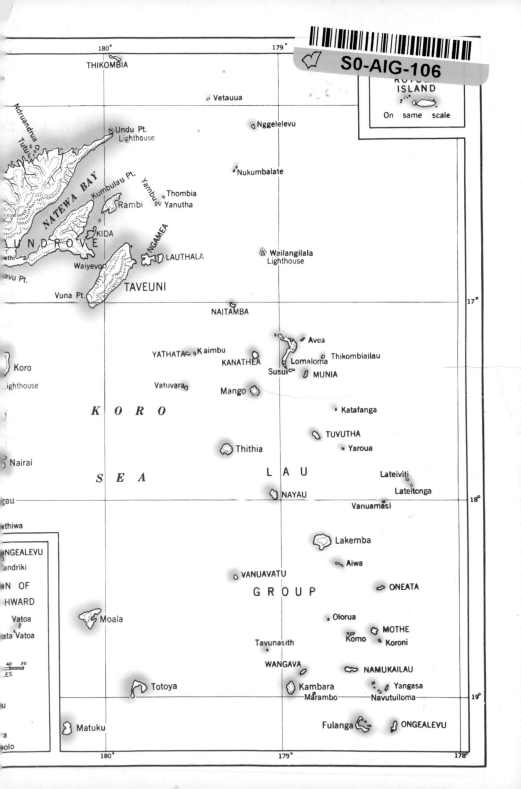

180° 179°

THIKOMBIA

ROTUMA
ISLAND
On same scale

Vetauua

Undu Pt.
Lighthouse

Nggelelevu

Mbuandrua

Tutu

NATEWA BAY

Kumbulau Pt.

Yambu Pt.

Thombia

Rambi

Yanutha

KIDA

NGAMEA

Waiyevo

LAUTHALA

Nukumbalate

Wailangilala
Lighthouse

Vuna Pt.

TAVEUNI

17°

NAITAMBA

Avea

Koro

Lighthouse

YATHATA

Kaimbu

KANATHEA

Lomaloma

Susui

MUNIA

Thikombiailau

Vatuvara

Mango

Katafanga

K O R O

TUVUTHA

Yaroua

Thithia

Nairai

S E A

L A U

Lateiviti

Lateitonga

au

NAYAU

Vanuamasi

18°

thiwa

NGEALEVU

andriki

Lakemba

Aiwa

N OF

HWARD

VANUAVATU

ONEATA

Vatoa

G R O U P

Olorua

ata Vatoa

Moala

MOTHE

Komo

Koroni

Tavunasith

WANGAVA

NAMUKAILAU

40   50
.ES

Totoya

Kambara

Marambo

Yangasa

Navutuiloma

19°

Matuku

Fulanga

ONGEALEVU

olo

180° 179° 178°

SO-AIG-106

The Drama of Fiji
A Contemporary History

FRONTISPIECE. One of the most important of the traditional customs still retained by the Fijians is the *yaqona* ceremony. *Yaqona* is the Polynesian *kava*, a root from which a drink is made. It is pronounced *yang-gona*. All photographs in this book by Rob Wright, Public Relations, Suva.

The DRAMA
of FIJI
A Contemporary History

by John Wesley Coulter

CHARLES E. TUTTLE CO.: PUBLISHERS
Rutland, Vermont & Tokyo, Japan

Representatives
Continental Europe: BOXERBOOKS, INC., *Zurich*
British Isles: PRENTICE-HALL INTERNATIONAL, INC., *London*
Australasia: PAUL FLESCH & CO., PTY. LTD., *Melbourne*
Canada: m.g. hurtig ltd., *Edmonton*

Published by the Charles E. Tuttle Company, Inc.
of Rutland, Vermont & Tokyo, Japan
with editorial offices at
Suido 1-chome, 2-6, Bunkyo-ku, Tokyo, Japan

Copyright in Japan, 1967 by Charles E. Tuttle Co., Inc.

Library of Congress Catalog Card No. 67-14279

First edition, 1967

Book design and typography by Keiko Chiba

Printed in Japan

To the Partridge family

Table of Contents

List of Illustrations

List of Tables

Preface

THE DRAMA OF FIJI is based on three periods of field-work in those islands at intervals over a period of twenty-three years, a visit to northern India, and relevant literature. The last visit to Fiji, in 1960, was part of a larger project in the South Pacific, made possible by a combined grant-in-aid of research, given by the Association of American Geographers and the Graduate School of the University of Cincinnati.

Middlebury, Vermont
January, 1967

Introduction

THE PROBLEM of colonialism in the Pacific is occupying the serious attention of Western governments. The rapid liquidation of that type of administration in the world in recent years has increased the mood of intolerance in the United Nations toward the remnants. The United States, Great Britain, France, and Australia have the responsibility for non-selfgoverning territories in the Pacific Ocean. Some of them are Trusteeships of the United Nations with which the author dealt when in the Pacific-Asia section of the Trusteeship Secretariat of that organization. New Zealand granted independence to its Trust Territory of Western Samoa in 1962. A Micronesian from the Marshall Islands, part of a Trust Territory administered by the United States, stated at a meeting of the Trusteeship Council in 1960: "The people of Africa and Asia are getting their freedom. We think we can do as good a job of governing ourselves as do those countries."

Fiji, Gilbert and Ellice Islands, and the Solomons archipelago in the Pacific are representative British colonies. Guam is an unincorporated territory of the United States;

American Samoa is incorporated. The people of these and other islands are moving toward self-government, some of them very slowly, others faster. Native populations are chafing at the bit, and Fiji and others are pushing hard for a greater share in their own administration.

In Fiji and in Tahiti, a French Territory, the situation is complicated by large alien populations, Indians in the former and Chinese in the latter. The colonists are willing to work much harder to develop the natural resources of the islands than the indigenous people, easy-going Melanesians and happy-go-lucky Polynesians. However in those archipelagoes there are few possibilities for further economic growth, and another difficulty to be overcome is the lack of capital for any developments which might be realized.

The problems of Fiji are tremendously complicated by the economic and political rivalry between the native Melanesians and tens of thousands of Indian colonists who are out to possess the land. The author had many opportunities to observe all phases of that rivalry during his residence in the archipelago. During my first period of fieldwork, in October and November 1937, I made many acquaintances among Fijians, Indians and Europeans who, in my study of the problems, were helpful then, and also on my later visits. On Fijian farms, where the operators were trying to break away from their traditional communal system of living, I observed their indifferent efforts at modern agriculture. A high point of that sojourn was a trip of several days with a high chief and an official of the Department of Agriculture into the interior of the island of Viti Levu to Nawanggambena village, in the vicinity of which the Fijians were raising bananas. They like that crop for, in their leisurely way, they can sit and watch it grow. Later on I was a guest of the chief in his home in Lomanikoro.

I stayed for three days with a Christian missionary to the Indians who was making little progress in converting them. He pointed out to me many attributes of that ethnic group which conflicted with characteristics of the indigenous people, most of whom are still little affected by modern progress. I watched the industrious people of Asia plow their sugar-cane fields carefully and engage actively in other aspects of agriculture. An interesting experience was to see an act of *Ramlila,* the epic story of the Hindu deities, Ram and Vishnu; the play was enacted evenings over a period of a week or so. Indian business and professional men in Suva talked with me about the economic situation in the islands. In rural "bazaars" and markets, salesmen offered me tourist wares between intervals of barter with the natives.

My second sojourn in Fiji, from November 1940 to January 1941, was on the *Cheng Ho,* a Chinese junk-yacht with a crew of eleven. I was a member of a scientific expedition with a botanist from the New York Botanical Gardens and a malacologist from Peabody Museum of Harvard University. That excursion was sponsored by Mrs. Archbold, the owner of the boat, who was on board. The advantage of that visit was to get to know parts of the archipelago seldom seen by anyone other than the indigenous population. In most places the Fijians were carrying on their traditional agriculture and ancient customs. In an isolated village, I and my companions tried to buy native artifacts, but the villagers refused to take money, for there was no store or shop within reach where they could spend it. We settled by bartering shirts we could spare.

This little volume draws on those two periods of field

work, on my last visit to the archipelago, in August 1960, and on research recently published. During the last visit I was impressed with the influence of the chiefs who were holding their biennial council. I had an opportunity to study and to discuss with some of my old friends the various factors which enter into the serious situation which exists in the colony. A solution of problems developing at the beginning of the last war seems to have reached an impasse. My information has been brought up to date by frequent correspondence, and *News from Fiji,* a goverment sponsored weekly publication.

The crisis in Fiji includes a good many circumstances, many of which are inter-related. They are nearly all included in the economic, political, and social ill-feeling which exists between people of a native Pacific-island culture and those of an Indian civilization. The two communities have wholly different attitudes and philosophies of life. The indigenous culture is that of a communally kin-based organization which restricts economic activity towards an individualistic way of living. On the other hand, the Indian attitude is that the chief ends of life are to be achieved by an individual's hard work. As well as having different senses of values, the two ethnic groups differ in language and religion.

An abortive attempt to establish the natives as independent farmers contributes to their dilemma. Peasant farming has never been carried on by any of the indigenous populations of the Pacific islands. Their economy has been a village cooperative system, in which the habits of peasant proprietors have no place. In a warm, rainy climate, where vegetation grows profusely, they come by food and shelter easily. Fijians would like nature to supply their wants without doing very much to help; they wish to keep large areas of land to use extensively and cooperatively. They despise the colonists, looking on them as usurpers who want to take away their land, and as people with whom they cannot compete, for they would have to work too hard. On the other hand, the Indians have settled on the land as individual farmers to work regularly, and market their produce under a system of money economy similar to that of Western countries. They want small farms to exploit intensively. They look down on the native population as people of an inferior culture.

The migration of the rural population of both groups to seek jobs in the towns causes a social problem. A serious situation in Tahiti, in North Africa, and in other countries has been brought about in a similar way, where the pressure of population on rural resources is heavily felt. The migrants generally live under conditions of very poor housing and sanitation. Since there is little they can do, with no opening for work, they are worse off in town and city than if they had remained in their villages.

A very important factor in Fiji is the persistent efforts of the ruling chiefs to preserve the ancient order, in which they have always held a privileged position. Commoners traditionally owed their chiefs allegiance, support in war, labor, and tribute of food and other material goods. The people always turned for advice and leadership to the ruling hierarchy. In the modern world in which the archipelago is now involved, the chiefs are incapable of leadership. A considerable number of young Fijians no longer want to do homage to the ruling class. They have had a good education, absorbed modern ideas, and in some cases have improved their economic status. Others who have traveled abroad return to the islands to become very dissatisfied with their lack of opportunity for advancement.

Indirect rule in Fiji has reinforced the position of the chiefs. It is an administration of native peoples in all parts of the world imposed by Western governments which did not have the competence or the knowledge to deal directly with their customs, traditions, and superstitions. Introduced into Fiji at the time of annexation by Great Britain, it has resulted in the existence of two separate governments in the archipelago, one for the natives and the other for the remaining ethnic groups. An attempt to interrelate them, and the unavoidable overlapping have resulted in confusion.

Indirect rule for the Colony of Fiji is likely to come to an end in the not distant future. The administration of native affairs through "Fijian Regulations" will have to be reoriented toward the gradual abandonment of the village system of communal society, for the policies and regulations of that kind of administration are inconsistent with the necessary encouragement of independent farming and regular work in other ways, both skilled and unskilled, which are necessary to improve the native standard of living. The Fijians themselves will have to be made more conscious of the fact that they must exert a great effort of readjustment.

A one-crop economy, sugar-cane farming, handicaps the agricultural development of the archipelago to its fullest extent. Except for brief periods, and for various reasons, the production of sugar there has gradually increased since 1900, but the great expansion in world production of that commodity has resulted in the imposition of a quota on Fiji, as well as on other countries growing that crop. The industry in Fiji has been developed almost exclusively by Indian labor. The Indians are commercial sugar-cane farmers, while the Fijians still practice their time-honored method of shifting cultivation.

Since there is no landlord-tenant act in the Colony, a farmer has to hand over a rented farm to the owner of the land when the lease expires, without compensation for improvements. Short term leases result in wasteful methods of exploiting the soil, for the lessee tries to get out of it as much as possible, regardless of the condition in which he hands it back.

Social problems include the policy of the government in maintaining segregated schools. Since the Fijians have had a distinct administration, it followed that they should have their own educational institutions. Furthermore they like that separation, for their children cannot compete successfully in academic endeavors with those of other ethnic groups. However, the system has tended to widen the gap between them and the Indians, and to make a reconciliation more difficult. The latter struggle for an education as hard as they work in the fields.

The government has not the financial resources necessary to provide educational facilities for all the children in the islands. There is a shortage of schools and teachers for thousands of children whose parents also lack an education. Christian missions play an important role in educating the Fijians. A considerable number of Indian schools are supported in whole or in part by societies and parents of that ethnic group. The schools for pupils of European ancestry are financed in part by them. The government maintains entirely only a few schools, but contributes to the support of many.

Factions and rivalries among the Indians prevent them from pulling together for the good of their adopted country.

Their contentions stem from differences in language, for the immigrants came from widely separated parts of the subcontinent which has a polyglot of tongues; from differences in occupation, for the business men, who come mostly from a restricted area of India—many of them in recent years—are jealous of their near-monopoly, stick together, and profit at the expense of the farmers; and from differences in religion—the great schism between Hindu and Muslim. Furthermore, political rivalries result in factions which increase dissension between the groups.

The increase in population, especially since World War II, in relation to the amount of land available for agriculture, and the lack of opportunities for earning a living in other ways, has made a solution of all these problems urgent. It is not that more children are born into families of the native people and those from India, but due to modern medicine and sanitation which have been introduced, more children live to grow up than formerly. In addition, Indians feed their children more intelligently than the indigenous people. Modern research in plant biology and in the management and mechanization of agricultural operations result in progressively fewer jobs for the rural population, and there is no parallel industrial development in the towns to employ them.

Because all these circumstances are common at present to many parts of the so-called "primitive" world, the author hopes that the book will have an appeal to readers interested in the liquidation of the remaining colonies, and especially to those who are students of the Pacific. The extraordinary thing is that there is a colony in that ocean where the natives do not want independence or even a full measure of self government.

PART I

The Milieu

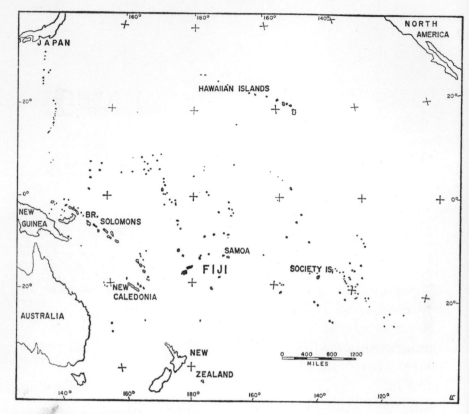

1. LOCATION OF FIJI IN PACIFIC OCEAN. Situated in the southwestern portion of the Pacific, the group of 503 islands (of which 106 are inhabited) is scattered over an area of 90,000 square miles. Fiji's isolated position has much to do with the products it can grow and sell at a profit.

CHAPTER 1

The Stage and the Scene

THE STAGE is set in 1964 in Fiji, a British Crown Colony in the southwest Pacific consisting of a group of 503 islands between latitudes 15° and 22° south of the equator, of which 106 are inhabited. The 180th meridian of longitude passes through the group. The islands are scattered over about 90,000 square miles of sea. The total land area of only 7,055 miles, part of which is estimated, is about six-tenths the size of Belgium, or a little smaller than the state of New Jersey. The main island, Viti Levu, constitutes more than half the area and has by far the largest number of people.

TABLE 1
AREAS OF MAIN ISLANDS

ISLAND	SQUARE MILES
Viti Levu	4010.79
Vanua Levu	2137.26
Taveuni	167.94
Kadavu	157.70

Eighteen other islands range from 54.2 square miles to 10.80 square miles.

The isolated position of Fiji in the southwest Pacific, and the natural environment of the archipelago, have an important bearing on what products can be grown and where they can be marketed at a profit. Suva, the capital and chief port is 1,960 miles from Sydney, 1,317 from Auckland, 3,183 from Honolulu, 5,611 from San Francisco, 11,590 miles from England via New York, and 13,280 via Sydney. It is, therefore, a long and expensive surface haul to markets for products which enter into world trade.

The mountainous nature of the larger islands restricts the area of land which can be successfully used for crops. Mount Victoria, the highest point on Viti Levu, reaches 4,550 feet; the highest peak on Vanua Levu is 3,437 feet, and on Taveuni, 4,040 feet. Many smaller units of land are coral formations varying from a few square yards to several square miles in area; they have little productive soil. Nearly all the islands in the group are surrounded either by fringing reefs or by barrier reefs, in the vicinity of which fishing is good. They form natural breakwaters from the ocean. Openings through them lead to safe and protected anchorages, and on the two larger islands, Viti Levu and Vanua Levu, to an intricate system of waterways navigated by small vessels engaged in coasting trade. The Rewa River, on Viti Levu, the longest waterway in Fiji, is navigable for flat-bottomed steamers for 80 miles from its mouth; several streams used by small craft flow into it. Among other large rivers, the Sigatoka and the Nadi drain the principal watersheds of Viti Levu. The Dreketi River on Vanua Levu is navigable for 15 miles from its mouth.

The climate, like that of most South Sea islands, is tradewind-oceanic. The amount and the distribution of rainfall have an important bearing on the sugar cane crop,

for sufficient moisture at the right time governs the amount of sugar in the stalk. The average annual total varies in well defined "wet" and "dry" zones from 140 to 60 inches. It extends over the whole year, but November to April is usually the wetter period. Excessive rainfall in some wet seasons is a serious difficulty, for although the river system of the archipelago is generally capable of carrying away heavy rain, at times the downpours are so great as to cause flooding and consequent damage to sugar cane and other crops, especially native produce for food. The more serious floods are associated with hurricanes which occur every four or five years, December to March being the months of greatest frequency. Fiji is in the hurricane belt of the Pacific, and a severe storm sometimes kills ten per cent of the coconut trees, and reduces the production of nuts from the survivors for many years (67, 21.)* The rainfall varies considerably from year to year and month to month, a fact also of considerable significance, for even a short drought in the tropics wilts growing vegetables. In August, 1963, a month before the South Pacific Games in Suva, the rainfall was some 40 inches, five times the average for that month (15). The Fijians, who love sports, looked out each morning with apprehension at the prospect of flooded playing fields.

Temperatures, ranging from a minimum of 59°F to a maximum of 96°, are modified from May to November by trade winds which, blowing regularly during those months, make life pleasant. Between December and April, when hot, northerly winds come from the equator, the mercury often rises to the 90's, and the humidity occasionally

---

* The first number refers to a reference at the back of the book with the corresponding number, the second to the page of that reference.

reaches the saturation point. Then the Fijians like to lie hour after hour in the shade, and the Indians work less vigorously.

The trade winds blow across the lowlands withholding most of their moisture to precipitate it copiously on the slopes of the mountains which lie across their path. The flat lands, except those cultivated, have a natural growth of grass. The windward slopes are clothed with a dense rain forest, broken only in the foothills by cultivated areas. The leeward elevations reflect particularly the dry season, for at that time the hillsides are covered with sparse grass, here and there with reeds, a few scattered shrubs, and drought-resistant trees. Extensive areas of mangrove forests, which skirt the coasts of the islands at the mouths of rivers, are of considerable importance as sources of fuel, and of wood for building native houses.

My first impression of Fiji was at the port of Suva in 1937, where stalwart Melanesians carried large wooden cases off our steamer. Turbaned East Indians strolled about the wharf stopping to look at the visitors arriving. Coming from the ship, and turning across Numbukalou Bridge into the town, I was struck by the cosmopolitan nature of the population: Fijians, Indians, Europeans, Chinese, Polynesians, and people of other ethnic groups. The mixture of races, creeds, languages, and customs is the outstanding feature of the population. It is the Oriental atmosphere which impresses the visitor most.

In the main shopping center, about the Triangle and along Victoria Parade, European and Indian shops display goods of interest to the local population and visitors alike. Brightly colored fabrics are piled high on counters and shelves of small shops with "Damodar," "Sital," "Akbar," and other Indian names in big letters above the doors and windows. In tailors' establishments and dressmakers' shops, Hindu men and women bend over yards of colored cloth, cutting and sewing. In grocery stores, sacks of turmeric and Indian pepper stand together, also bags of betel nuts, and containers of little dried fish and ingredients of curry. Women in long, flowing saris walk about with little ornaments in their noses.

Bearded Sikhs and older Indians in dhoties add to the Oriental scene. Occasionally a stately Fijian man with head erect, dressed in a shirt and knee-length skirt or *sulu,* walks with dignity through the main thoroughfare.

The scene in the countryside varies from place to place. In many parts of the lowlands, neat rectangular sugar cane farms occupy the landscape. Smoke belches from the chimney of a sugar mill which towers above lines of small frame dwellings partly screened by leafy trees. The farmers and workers about the mill are Indians. A European in a small automobile drives about, surveying the quality of the cane. Here and there an Indian is working in a rice field. In the rolling country inland, and especially in the river valleys, the thatched huts of native villages bespeak a peaceful atmosphere, removed from the turmoil of the modern world. In the hill country, isolated tribes live much as they did 100 years ago, using digging sticks for spades. In both lowlands and highlands, a large cane knife is used for everything from felling a tree to peeling yams. Fijian men and women wear *sulu,* wrapped around the hips and tucked in at the left side.

Near each village are the food gardens in which are grown the vegetables and fruit that form the major part of the native diet. Fowls and pigs scratch and root about in the vicinity.

The following table gives the population of the archipel-

TABLE 2

POPULATION, 1956		POPULATION, 1962	
European	6,402	European	10,553
Part-European	7,810	Part-European	9,226
Chinese & Part-Chinese	4,155	Chinese & Part-Chinese	5,177
Rotuman	4,422	Rotuman and other Pacific Islanders	12,179
Other Pacific Islanders	5,320	Fijian	177,770
Fijian	148,134	Indian	212,828
Indian	169,403	All Others	117
All Others	91		
TOTAL	345,737	TOTAL	427,850

ago in the census of 1956 and in 1962 (officially estimated). The Europeans in Fiji dominate several industries and professions. They staff sugar mills, large business firms, banks and government offices most of which are located in the towns, where 79 per cent of them live (20, 10). Half of them, engaged in commerce, are concerned with wholesale and retail trade and distribution. Those in the country are predominantly owners or managers of copra plantations and cattle farms. The European population is largely a temporary group—people who will retire to New Zealand, Australia or England, their home countries, when they have served their terms in business or government. A few hundred Europeans are permanent settlers, children and grandchildren of families who have lived in the colony for three or four generations. Many of them, interrelated by marriage, form social groups of their own.

The part-Europeans are nearly all descendants of Europeans and Fijians. Their forbears were European traders and shipwrights who took wives from among the native population. The descendants, with special aptitudes for

ETHNIC COMPOSITION OF THE POPULATION OF FIJI 1901-1962

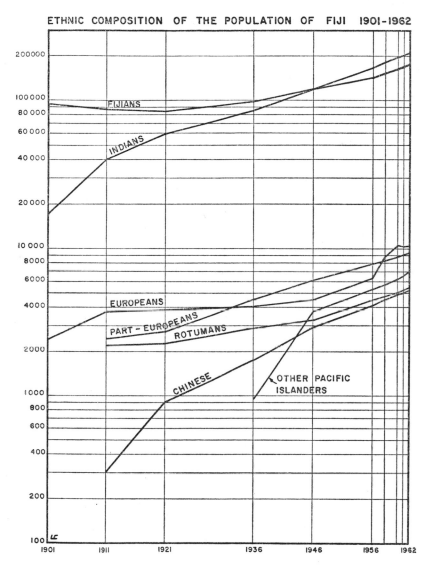

3. ETHNIC COMPOSITION OF THE POPULATION OF FIJI (1901–1962). The conglomeration of races, creeds, languages, and customs is one of the outstanding features of the populace, and first-time visitors are usually surprised by the cosmopolitan nature of the islanders.

shipbuilding and sailing, have made careers in those fields. Some of them, born on coconut plantations are among leading copra planters today. Others capably fill positions in various kinds of business, many as clerks in the larger trading firms, and in government service (27, 134).

Chinese have been coming to Fiji since the last quarter of the 19th century, and in considerable numbers since World War II. They engage mainly in trading, operating stores in towns where two-thirds of them live; some are market gardeners and others raise pigs and poultry. They are good citizens of the Colony and many of them have taken Fijian wives (53, 159).

The other Pacific Islanders in Fiji have come at various periods. Some of them were imported in the early years of economic development to work on sugar cane and coconut plantations. Before Fiji became a British colony, the demand of European settlers for labor was met by the introduction of people from the Solomon Islands, the New Hebrides, the Gilberts and other island groups. Settlements of Solomon Islanders near Suva, Levuka and Labasa include many descendants of these early people (27, 136). The natives of the other archipelagoes have been integrated to some extent with the indigenous population.

The indigenous people are Melanesians with a marked though variable Polynesian strain, which is strong in the eastern islands, but much less apparent in the west and in the interiors of the main islands. Many of the hill tribes are pure-blooded Melanesians (3, 73). Eastern Fiji is a frontier where two streams of migration, Melanesians from the west and Polynesians from the east, met and mingled (31, 4, 27, 122). The Fijians are mainly subsistence farmers, concerned with the production of food crops. About 90 per cent of them live in villages near which their gardens provide yams, taro, cassava (tapioca), *kumala* (sweet potatoes), and other vegetables and fruit. During the past three or four decades their population has considerably increased— from 84, 475 in 1921 to 157, 808 in 1958.

The Indians earn a living mainly in sugar cane farming, but also by raising rice and other vegetables. They, with the Chinese, have almost a monopoly of the retail trade outside of Suva. Many of them have entered professions. The great majority were born in the islands and have never seen the land of their fathers; they consider themselves as much natives of Fiji as the Fijians themselves. From a background of frugality and industry, in the rigorous social and economic environment of rural India, they have improved very much their status in an undeveloped British colony in the mid-Pacific. Eighty-one per cent of them live in the country (20, 10).

It is with the ethnic conflict between the Fijians and Indians that this book deals, between a people nurtured by nature, easygoing, kindly, and hospitable, like those of all the Pacific islands, and others of an aggressive, Asian culture, born of adversity into a highly competitive economic environment. The attributes of hard work, industry, and thrift passed on to their children and grandchildren in Fiji bid fair to drive the native people to the wall.

The Indian population is increasing at a rate which fills the Fijians with alarm. They now represent approximately 50 per cent of the total population of the Colony and the Fijians, about 43 per cent.

PART II

The Fijians

CHAPTER 2

The Background of the Fijians

BEFORE FIJI was ceded to the British Crown, in 1874, the indigenous population had been considerably disturbed by the advent of Europeans. People from Great Britain, Australia, and New Zealand, who had settled in the islands, purchased tracts of land from the chiefs—some of it under dubious circumstances. They had been bringing in workers from neighboring archipelagoes for sugar cane and copra plantations. It was chiefly to end abuses in importing labor that Great Britain annexed the islands (27, 136).

In 1874, the Government of Cakobau, the strongest chief in the archipelago, was in dire straits financially, and faced with many other problems. Cakobau offered, for the third time, to cede Fiji to Great Britain. Unlike the previous offers, this one was unconditional, with the exception that some lands were to be reserved to the Fijians, as provided in Clause 4 of the Deed of Cession (26, 234).

In 1879, five years after the Deed of Cession was consummated, an event occurred which, as years went on, was to change the whole economic and social situation in the islands. That was the importation of 481 laborers from

India. They came under a system of indenture for five years to any plantation, sugar cane or copra, to which they were assigned, and after that they were free to work for anybody or in any way they pleased. The influx of immigrants continued and gathered momentum towards the last part of that century. It continued during the early part of the 20th, and by 1917 free settlers represented a large part of the Indian population in the colony (27, 138). They were engaged mostly in agriculture, either on small areas of land of their own, or on those leased from European sugar companies or from other Europeans, who then owned considerable real estate in the islands. The impact of the Indian culture had a profound effect on the Fijians, who, all through the years, had remained as subsistence farmers on the land of their tribes.

Native Agriculture

At the time of the cession of the archipelago, the traditional way of living of the indigenous population was something like that in the Pacific islands in general. It is still carried on today, modified, however, by the impact of Western and Asian cultures. The customs of Fijian society entailed certain mutual obligations between members of a family or village group. An important feature was the common ownership of land by cognate social units. Traditionally the land-owning unit was the *i'tokatoka,* a small collection of families related by marriage. Various family groups amongst whom there had been intermarriage collectively formed a *mataqali*. The *yavusa,* a larger social unit, was a combination of several *mataqali* (20, 37).

The Fijian had no conception of the individual ownership of land, or indeed of the outright ownership of pro-

4. FIJIAN FARMER IN FIELD OF PEANUTS, SIGATOKA. The indigenous people, of Melanesian origin, are mainly subsistence farmers, concerned wiith the production of food crops. Peanuts are only one of several agricultural exports of Fiji.

5. FIJIAN TOBACCO FARMERS. An important feature of native agriculture is the common ownership of land by cognate social units made up of various family groups amongst whom there had been intermarriage.

perty. "To him what we should class as goods and chat-
tels, his land or even his own body, was his only so long as
he could retain it. He might if he could and would take
any such property from another entirely without impro-
priety; nor would he resist, or even wish to resist the taking
from himself of any such property by any one who could
and would take it" (37, 262).

The method of agriculture for the indigenous people was
to clear or partially clear a portion of forest or other land
not far from the villages in which they lived. They chopped
down the trees, cutting them off three or four feet from the
ground with bush knives introduced by traders, leaving the
heavier branches where they fell. They planted taro and
other crops with digging sticks. After two or three years,
when the soil was exhausted, the area was abandoned for
a new clearing which was used in the same way. In, say
ten or a dozen years, the soil had recuperated; the old plot
was recleared, and the process repeated. That method of
agriculture is still carried on in the islands today.

Nearly all the plants grown by the Fijians are indigenous
in the Pacific. Several varieties of taro are raised but that
most prized is a variety called *dalo* in Fijian, *boka* in some
islands. Yams have always been an important food. For
them the ground has to be carefully prepared. Several
varieties are commonly eaten: one, *daunini* to the Fijians;
another, a white yam with a red skin—*vurai* in the native
language (48). A third variety is prized in part because it
grows very large. The tubers are long and cylindrical, and
as thick as a man's arm. I ate a cooked piece of one three
feet long and ten inches in diameter. After hurricanes which
destroy village crops, the wild yam, *tikau* to the natives, is
very valuable for food. It grows in the forest, the vines
trailing in graceful festoons over trees and shrubs.

6. GREATER YAM *(dioscorea alata)*. This is a twining vine, commonly cultivated in the Pacific. Yams vary enormously in shape and size, some of them weighing up to 30 pounds. The yam is an excellent food, baked or boiled, and an important part of the native diet.

Cassava is a shrub six to eight feet tall, the tubers of which furnish a starch, our tapioca. Introduced into the archipelago many years ago, it is now widely grown by Fijians. The plant takes from twelve to fifteen months to come to maturity.

The potato was introduced into the Pacific, we think, from the American continent. The voyage of the *Kon Tiki* proved that contacts between South America and the eastern islands of Polynesia were possible. Generally speaking, however, the indigenous vegetation of Fiji has a strong Indo-Malayan element (47, 18). Large quantities of sweet potatoes *(kumala)* are raised; they constitute one of the main articles of the native diet, grow well on grassy plains where the soil is sandy. The dried root of the kava plant when ground, is macerated with water to form the native beverage common to many Pacific islands. In Fiji, where considerable land is devoted to it, it is called *yaqona*.

From earliest times the coconut palm has furnished food and drink for the people of nearly all the Pacific islands; it provides materials for building houses, cordage, baskets and much else besides. It grows and fruits for a hundred years, but from 70 or 80 years on, the fruits are few and small. Three or four generations of people may gather nuts every month from a healthy palm. Copra, the dried meat, traded for its oil, is one of the more important articles of commerce in the Pacific.

Breadfruit is also widely distributed. The tree, 70 feet high, bears spherical fruit five or six inches in diameter. There are several species in Fiji which have one name in common, *bucotabua*. The long leaves of the pandanus tree, *varawa*, are the most important materials for making floor mats and sleeping mats. Groves of this plant flourish among forest swamps in the interior of the two larger islands. Mats are also made from a variety called *balawa* (48). The largest tree in the forest, *dakua makadre* in Fijian, one of the *Coniferae,* once very plentiful, was very valuable not only for its timber but also for its gum; there are few specimens left (48).

Many other plants were, and still are important in the Fijian native economy. The juices of several including *vutu* are used to stupefy fish. *Yabiadina,* found everywhere in the archipelago, and often referred to erroneously as arrowroot, is favored as a food and is also much used in medicine for dysentery and diarrhea. *Bahonga,* a fern, is given by mothers to their children when they have indigestion. An infusion of *coboi* or lemon grass is generally used for tea, and, when dried, is often the stuffing for pillows. The juice of the leaves of *vakeke,* a variety of hibiscus, has been traditionally used by women to produce sterility (48).

The Social System

The native is born into a social system in which the unit and heart of the organization is the *mataqali* or clan, "a kind of enlarged family, where all the elders are fathers, and all the juniors are children. Family relationships are not very clearly differentiated from clan relationships" (25, 100).

All the larger works in a village are carried out by clan labor. When a house is to be built, craftsmen of the clan perform the work under the direction of a local chief. Members of the kin go out together to mend a trail impaired for travel by heavy rains. In every other undertaking of importance, the group does it collectively.

The Fijians developed a predilection for working cooperatively. The habit of doing things together became an integral part of a native's life, and of his way of thinking—clearing land for agriculture, growing food for visitors, cutting logs for canoes, and building them. All the cooperative-communal duties are referred to as *lala,* done at the command of a chief. Personal *lala* are the services and goods demanded by the ranking man from an individual, including the choicest products of the harvest. Fishing is also a cooperative undertaking; besides a share of the catch, all turtles caught are handed over to the chief. This activity was formerly much more important than now.

The nature of the communal way of life on which the village society is based discourages the production of food above the level of a subsistence economy. Indeed there is no necessity for an individual to cultivate any part of the tribally-owned land beyond the point of furnishing his immediate needs; it supplies all that is required for his simple wants. He never has to struggle for a living, and there is no such thing as poverty. Furthermore, he has plenty of time on his hands to be, from a Western point of view, indolent and lazy.

Customary obligations of village life include great effort and expenditure on the occasion of births, marriages and deaths, especially when these occur in a family of high rank. Elaborate preparations are made, including building temporary houses to accommodate guests from other villages. Great piles of native food are lavishly displayed. The ceremonial drinking of *yaqona* is an essential part of all of them. In Fijian formal assemblies it has great socio-psychological value. It is a focus of communal life and an important factor in sustaining it (55, 51).

As among most so-called "primitive" people, the dance *(meke),* one of their principal amusements, often accompanies feasts. On occasions of rejoicing it is generally well organized. Ballet dances are generally performed by large groups. The sitting dance, now often done, was introduced from Polynesia (38, 104). All these forms of diversion are mimetic. One of them, performed in my honor, at the behest of a high chief, my host in a village, was a sitting dance describing in pantomine the journey of natives who went to London to represent the Colony at the Coronation of King George VI: a boat with two chimneys; the voyage; arrival at Westminster Abbey, and placing crowns on the heads of the king and queen. The most vigorous and exciting dance from the point of view of the participants and spectators, too, is a war dance, done by men in their martial make up; it depicts surprise, skirmishes, and victory.

Fijians depend on their chiefs for guidance in all matters, great and small. A commoner never has had to think for himself, for his work has always been directed under the communal system. Even the planting of food crops on which his very existence depends has been a matter for guidance by authority (16, 15). Absolute reliance upon those above him in rank played a large part in the formation of the native's character. The chief decided how many taro tops he should plant, the number of yams he must grow, and the sweet potatoes necessary for his own family and for village feasts. Among considerations binding a chief to his people was their common ownership of land. Although the first fruits of the harvest were formerly presented to him, they were in fact shared by his people. A chief was required to exercise strong leadership both in peace and in war. The power vested in him was exercised, for example, in one of his privileges, namely, summoning the clansmen together at a moment's notice. His actions on behalf of his tribal unit were those expected of a man ruling not by right of hereditary status alone, but by his ability to lead. His power depended on the goodwill of the governed, and it was the most suitable candidate, not necessarily the next in seniority, who was ceremonially installed in the position of paramount chief (51, 68, 94).

An inflexible custom of native society—one may say an inexorable law, is the traditional observance of *kere kere,* a form of ceremonial begging. It is a practice of "borrowing" from a kinsman at the will of a borrower. If a man has more salt than he wants, his more needy neighbors "beg" it from him. If he needs yams for his daughter's marriage feast, he has a claim on each of them. It is an inviolable law of property that a man can obtain something he wants from a more affluent kinsman. He cannot think of refusing any of his possessions to one who importunes them by *kere kere,* consoling himself with the reflection that the benefaction affords him a claim on the borrower at some future time (57, 80). Personal ownership of property is a custom generally restricted to things that are used by members of a man's family: floor mats, sleeping mats, and implements for agriculture or fishing—objects which might be described as craft products. But even these are sometimes "begged" by relatives and friends (51, 36).

Land Situation in the Colony

While the Fijians carried on their traditional culture including their way of farming, the land situation in the islands as it affected them was becoming more and more acute. The Deed of Cession was regarded by them, and still is held to be, a guarantee of their racial identity and especially of the ownership of their lands (16, 17). In 1880 a Land Commission, on evidence argued before it, had allowed the alienation of about 415,000 acres to European settlers who had "purchased" land from native chiefs; it was a large part of the more productive area of the archipelago. A few years before that, sales of native lands beyond those already made were prohibited, but leaseholds were granted for a term not to exceed 21 years. The short-term lease was not conducive to rapid settlement, and, during the next 20 years, only 100 leases were issued for a total of some 13,000 acres (41, 2). Of that area, 7,000 acres were taken up for sugar cane plantations and 4,000 for timber.

Owing to the repeated requests of Europeans and Indians, a Native Land Ordinance of 1905 permitted the sale of land by the natives. The area sold during the four years between 1905 and 1909 equalled 20,184 acres. In 1912 an Amending Ordinance prohibited the further alienation of land except to the government. The Native Land Trust Ordinance of 1940 marked an important step in the land situation. Its objectives were: (a) The protection of the native interest in their own soil, and the reservation of an area ample for their needs at that time and in the future; (b) the provision of suitable and sufficient land for settlement by others; and (c) the achievement of continuity of policy of tenure and the security of leaseholds (21, 53 ff; 41, 2). A Native Lands Commission was set up to determine and demarcate native reserves. This identification of the land of the indigenous people is continuing. A Native Land Trust Board, set up under the Commission, controls the establishment of land reserved for the Fijians, and the leasing of other Fijian land (4, 131).

Table 3 gives the figures for land tenure in the Fiji Islands in 1959.

TABLE 3
LAND TENURE IN FIJI
ACRES

Fijian tribal land	3,756,000	(of which about 312,000 acres are leased)
Fijian freehold	12,000	
Crown freehold	75,000	
European and Indian freehold and other	534,000	
Crown Schedule A	120,000	(land of extinct *mataquali*)
Crown Schedule B	88,000	(unclaimed at Cession)
	4,585,000	

Of the 312,000 acres of Fijian land on lease, 27,000 are to the Government; it controls in all, 317,000 acres (55, 16).

The indigenous population then owns about 83.5 per cent of the total land area of the Colony; of that amount 91.5 per cent is unalienated by lease (55, 1). However, those figures do not give a correct impression of the real situation in regard to agriculture. It is important to note that one-half of the total area of the archipelago, amounting to 2,050,860 acres, is unsuitable for almost anything.

Only 1,016,901 acres can be successfully used, including land for tree crops, grazing, and also productive forest land (21, 53 ff.). Fifty-five per cent of the relatively small amount of good arable land on Viti Levu is alienated by freehold or by lease (55, 1). Indeed by far the greater part of Fijian-owned land is of little value for agriculture; the natives use some of it for their traditional shifting cultivation, other acres for grazing, and a considerable area for gathering reeds, yams and similarly wild products. Only about 8.4 per cent of the total land area of Fiji is cultivated and of that, 35 per cent is used by Fijians.

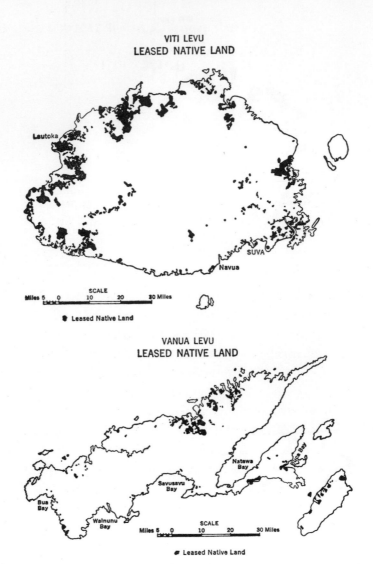

VITI LEVU
LEASED NATIVE LAND

Lautoka

SUVA
Navua

SCALE
Miles 5   0   10   20   30 Miles

● Leased Native Land

VANUA LEVU
LEASED NATIVE LAND

Natewa
Bay

Savusavu
Bay

Bua
Bay

Wainunu
Bay   SCALE
                Miles 5   0   10   20   30 Miles

● Leased Native Land

8. LEASED NATIVE LAND ON VANUA LEVU AND VITI LEVU. The indigenous population owns about 83.5 per cent of the total land area of the Colony; of this, about 91.5 per cent is unalienated by lease. Unfortunately, by far the great portion of Fijian-owned land is of little value for agriculture. More than half of the small amount of good arable land on Viti Levu is alienated by freehold or lease. (Courtesy, Burns Report, pp. 20, 21.)

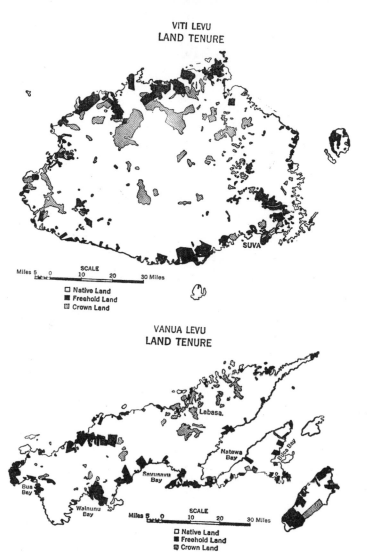

VITI LEVU
LAND TENURE

SCALE
Miles 5   0   10   20   30 Miles

□ Native Land
■ Freehold Land
▨ Crown Land

SUVA

VANUA LEVU
LAND TENURE

Labasa

Natewa Bay

Bica Bay

Savusavu Bay

Bua Bay

Walnunu Bay

SCALE
Miles 5   0   10   20   30 Miles

□ Native Land
■ Freehold Land
▨ Crown Land

9. LAND TENURE. The Native Land Trust Ordinance of 1940 marked an important step in the land situation. Its objectives were the protection of the native interest in their own soil and the keeping of ample reservations of land for their present and future use; provision for suitable and sufficient land for settlement by others; and the achievement of a continuity of policy in land tenure and for the security of the leaseholder. (Courtesy, Burns Report, pp. 17, 18).

TABLE 4
ARABLE LAND (55, 1)

	ACRES
Total land area	4,500,000
Unstable steepland soils (Part of it usable for tree crops)	3,650,000
Arable land (including swamps)	850,000

The most important single landholder in Fiji is the Colonial Sugar Refining Company, commonly referred to as the CSR. It secured land very early in the history of the colony, and from time to time acquired the holdings of other companies and those of private sugar cane planters. At present it operates three large sugar mills, and supervises the plantations and farms which they serve. It owns 75,000 acres, most of which is leased to Indian sugar cane farmers.

The fact that the better lands of the archipelago are owned or worked by Europeans and Indians, and the leaseholds of the latter—all of the areas being used in a system of farming entirely unfamiliar to the indigenous people— gives the Fijians considerable concern, is especially objectionable to their chiefs, and constitutes the most serious problem of the government of the colony.

CHAPTER 3

Peasant Farmers

THE ALIENATION of land for commercial agriculture, and the success of the Indians as independent farmers, prompted private individuals interested in the welfare of the native population, and also the Government of the Colony, to try to establish Fijians on their land as individual agriculturalists.

The first attempt on a fairly large scale was made by a Methodist missionary, Rev. A.D. Lelean, in the early '30's. He told me that he sought to settle individuals on small sugar cane plots, each doing his own work, but combining their efforts at harvest time. His efforts, however, seem to have been fruitless and are now lost in obscurity (55, 86). The Director of Agriculture of the colony stated to me in 1937, "Under the prevailing communal system of the Fijians, there is no incentive for them to be industrious as they can claim no ownership of the fruits of their labors, and hence efforts to introduce individualism are being made so that it may be possible for the natives to take an interest in their own progress." The Colonial Sugar Refining Company entered into the scheme to help the indigenous population to establish itself economically, leasing some of its land to Fijian tenants.

It was arranged through the Government that a Fijian wishing to become an independent farmer *(galala)* on a piece of land belonging communally to his *mataqali* or tribal unit, or wanting to lease land from the CSR, could do it provided he fulfilled certain obligations towards his chief, his village and his kinsfolk. He could commute his services to a chief by a fixed annual payment in money or in kind, and, by additional payments, he could be absolved from mending the trails of his province, thatching houses in his village, or rendering any of the other social services for which he was liable. He had to manage his holding by sound agricultural methods or his commutation could be cancelled. That method of establishing natives as individualists is practiced today.

The Fijians who raise sugar cane, work under the immediate supervision of the Colonial Sugar Refining Company. They live in native huts with walls of bamboo framework thatched with leaves of sugar cane or grass; the dirt floor is covered with reeds. A door or a wooden shutter in each wall for a window lets in light and air. A dwelling is the temporary home of two or three young men away from their tribal villages. The company gives them credit for various supplies and services rendered during the growing season: seed, fertilizer, and use of machinery. I visited a small group of Fijian cane farmers who owned a horse in common which they used for plowing. They joined together to cut the crop cooperatively and the company hauled it to the mill. Despite the best efforts of the CSR, however, the Fijian share of the total acreage of cane and their output of sugar is only about five per cent of the total (55, 3).

Some of the individual farmers grow coconuts for copra, but a large part of that product is raised cooperatively on *mataqali* land. Raising coconut palms does not require much labor, nevertheless the copra is of very poor quality. The groves are neglected and allowed to grow up in weeds. Many old trees bear little fruit and should be replaced by seedlings. The product is for the most part sun-dried, although it would not be difficult to procure inexpensive hot-air driers to be used cooperatively. When the market price of copra is low, the Fijians lose any incentive to care for the trees or gather the ripe nuts. The average production of copra from Fijian groves is about 460 pounds per acre compared with 550 pounds from other coconut lands (4, 195).

Growing bananas under a communal system is also an important native enterprise. I saw land recently prepared for that fruit, cleared in the same way as for taro and yams. Trees were cut two or three feet from the ground, the stumps left standing and logs lying about. Shoots from an old banana root were planted among the stumps and logs, to mature in from nine to twelve months, each bearing one large stand of fruit. Programs of work for a number of villages in central Viti Levu take into account that many villagers are occupied with that crop, and their communal work in the village is scheduled in relation to its cultivation.

The principal areas of growing bananas on Viti Levu include the valleys of the Rewa River and its tributaries, the Tailevu and Navua and also the district of Sigatoka. Unfortunately the quality of the fruit is poor, and that branch of farming is not in a satisfactory condition. The soil used near the villages is in general exhausted, and the natives have to walk farther and farther to new ground.

They waste time in getting to the plantations and have less time to work when they get there. They neglect especially the use of insecticides (55, 4). When the fruit is ready to ship, they load it for Suva on bamboo rafts which they call "no come back boats," for, at the end of the trip, they sell the bamboo for lumber and walk home. The greatest disadvantage is their entire dependence on an uncertain market in New Zealand to which ships go irregularly.

Growing *yaqona* is a profitable crop most of which is produced by Fijians. As already mentioned, the preparation of the root and drinking the infusion hold an important place in native culture. The plant takes from four to six years to mature and harvesting is slow. Processing merely entails cutting up the root and drying it. *Yaqona* is a crop which, although widely raised in small quantities, is ideally suited to the people in the hills. It requires initial effort and enthusiasm, but can then be left unattended, being sold at any time from four to five years later. "If they need money, they take the *yaqona* down to the more sophisticated areas on horseback and sell it; if there is no immediate need for money, they stay at home and drink it!" (10, 5).

Some Fijians near the towns engage to some extent in market gardening. I saw several who had been given about one-fifth of an acre by their chief on which to grow rice, taro, tapioca or European vegetables which they could sell. If they were successful in these small ventures, he told me, he had promised them farms of two or three acres.

Individual farming for the indigenous population has not been a success. As a whole there are only about 1,300 natives who are attempting it (55, 90). It engages 3.5 per cent of Fijians who pay taxes, and about 5.5 per cent of all those engaged in cropping enumerated in the census of

10. BAMBOO RAFTS laden with bananas are poled down a river to a packing station where the banana fingers are stripped from bunches and packed for shipment overseas.

11. SACKS OF COPRA—dried kernel of the coconut—are loaded onto
a freighter to be milled to produce coconut oil.

12. FIJIAN SAILING canoes are constructed from hollowed logs and equipped with sails from woven pandanus leaves.

13. A TYPICAL Fijian village site is selected for its accessibility to a waterway, proximity to fertile land and fresh water, and where it receives maximum protection from the weather.

1956. In short, of 63.6 per cent of adult Fijian men engaged in agricultural and pastoral activities, only eight per cent of them have broken away from the traditional pattern of village subsistence production to engage either as proprietors, employees, or individuals in specialized agriculture and grazing (20, 44).

A number of Fijians try to raise cattle, but since keeping these animals had no place in their traditional economy, efforts to introduce stock farming have met with little success. On coconut plantations the animals serve a useful purpose by grazing on grass, weeds, and other undergrowth, and so keep the ground cleared among the palms. But the natives kill them off one by one for their feasts. Even when they have had a few dairy cows which furnished milk for their children, the number was depleted at the first celebration.

About 600 Fijians engage in forestry, lumbering, and saw milling—out of a total of 1,000 employed in that industry. However, half of those in the proprietary and managerial grades are Indians and most of the rest Europeans (55, 73). Fifty per cent of the colony's total area is covered with forest which is principally tropical rain forest occupying the wet windward slopes of the large islands. However, reckless clearing for plantations or gardens by the natives, and indiscriminate felling for house timber, have ruined much good woodland. They commonly burn tree-covered land to get wild yams more easily, but sometimes such destruction is "apparently merely wanton" (55, 73).

There is almost an entire neglect of fishing by the native population, although the ocean about the islands abounds in life. Barracuda and albacore are plentiful in off-shore waters; giant cod run to several hundred pounds. Outside the main reef, dolphin and bonito are taken, as well as swordfish (12, 129). Although the Fijians are very strongly attached to coastal fishing rights, there are nearly as many Indians as natives in this poorly nourished infant industry (55, 74). Women and children fish in shallow water on the reefs to get part of the family food supply.

Work in gold mines is reserved for Fijians as far as is practicable. The Tavua area, the most important mining district in the archipelago, is six miles from the north coast of Viti Levu. The settlement there, known as Vatukoula, is one of the larger outside of Suva. The indigenous population constitutes from 55 to 60 per cent of the labor force—about 900 workers out of a total of 1,600 in this industry (55, 71). Residential areas for the natives have been carefully planned and amenities provided on a liberal scale. For Fijian employees and their families, the mining companies have taken pains to reproduce, as far as possible, the favorable environment of the native village.

In 1956 Fijians numbered 300 out of 419 people engaged in any capacity in manganese mining. They accounted for five of the 37 proprietary, managerial, and executive positions (55, 72). Men working for wages were selected, giving the natives preferential consideration.

Large numbers of Fijians are employed by the administration in various departments, and also in the police force. Almost all those professionally trained, except clergymen, are in government service. The natives dominate as stevedores, an occupation in which they have an advantage over the Indians because of their large, strong physiques. Fijian women predominate in nursing; in that profession, their rate is 523 to 65 Indian women. A considerable number of female native workers are domestic servants (55, 74–75).

The following table gives the number of Fijians who are non-agricultural laborers (55, 71). They are for the most part unskilled.

TABLE 5
FIJIAN WAGE EMPLOYEES

YEAR	NUMBER OF FIJIAN WAGE EMPLOYEES	PERCENTAGE OF TOTAL WAGE EMPLOYEES
1954	8,664	41.8
1955	9,015	41.5
1956	9,881	42.8
1957	10,053	43.4

The natives are very unsuccessful in business as well as in independent farming, and, there are only about a score who try to operate stores or shops in the islands.

Despite the encouragement and help given to Fijians to engage in individual farming, and notwithstanding the preferences afforded them for employment in the lumber industry, in mining, and other kinds of work, the indigenous population has been unsuccessful in changing the traditional way of living to meet the competitive demands of the modern world. As businessmen they have signally failed. Various reasons are adduced to explain the situation. Europeans in the islands commonly alleged to the author, "Fijians are tropically lazy and have little intention of working regularly, let alone hard." Others said, "Because of their lack of initiative, the natives have the prospect of only a low standard of living." However, their standard of living is high according to my observations in India and China, but low compared with what I saw in Tahiti and New Caledonia. Fijians themselves have many ready excuses for not working. They say, "It's too warm to work hard." One of them remarked to me, "This is a beautiful day so why waste it working." Another, "We have too far to walk to our copra plantations."

In justice to the indigenous people, it must be stated

that they work hard in groups for brief periods, in short bursts, with long intervals of rest in between. A Fijian is enthusiastic if he is allowed to throw in his lot with his fellows. During World War II, in a friendly contest with American soldiers in speed of unloading freight at Suva, the Fijians won. They love the rough and tumble of a rugby game and the lasting effort it demands. They have even been known to work regularly for a spurt of eight or nine days on a European copra plantation tempted by a bonus, but then they generally quit and went home to their village.

In view of the fact that the chiefs have lost much of their old power to compel the natives to plant sufficient quantities of the proper crops, they tend to raise only those which require the least effort. Fewer yams are raised now than formerly for they need more care than other crops. They have to be "hilled," and poles must be provided up which the vines climb. On some sugar cane farms I visited, the Fijian operators, who were growing their own food, were raising cassava almost exclusively. It is necessary merely to stick a piece of the stem of that plant in the ground, and in from six months to a year or two, the tubers will be large enough to harvest, boil, or bake, and eat; the longer in the soil, the larger the edible underground stems.

Natives cannot accept routine as an element in any kind of work, whether in employment away from the village, or even in such tasks as feeding an infant at regular intervals, or milking a cow twice a day (51, 82) "Fijians abhor punctuality. Fixed routine in daily life is unknown to them; their functions are controlled only by the impulse of the moment; they have never learned to put a value on time; they have never a thought for the remote future;

system of any kind is peculiarly irksome. When a Fijian has attempted to keep cattle, he has shown that he would rather let his beasts die of thirst than be bound by the necessity of giving them water at stated intervals" (57, 229). Fijian sugar cane farmers can be persuaded to plow their land and plant it properly. But it seems impossible to get them to look after the crop as it grows; they will not hoe it or weed it. The head teacher of the Cakaudrove Provincial Training Farm told me it was very difficult to get the boys to be on time for meals, and to work regularly at a fixed hour every day.

Since most of the necessities of life are produced without difficulty in every village, the attitude of the people seems to be that nature will supply their wants without much effort on their part. They still hanker after the large areas for farming that they had in the old days, and want to use them for shifting agriculture by rotating the land instead of the crop. The native individual farmer cannot easily overlook the advantages of the traditional cooperative communal system, which provided for everybody for the period of his life. He asks himself, "Who will look after me when I am old or ill or for some reason unable to work?" In his way of thinking, there is no provision for accident or enforced unemployment. He must face the risks of sickness, domestic calamity, and old age. He is reluctant to be "independent" in the modern sense of European culture. The Colonial Sugar Refining Company has established Fijians on sugar cane farms already prepared for planting, only to see them drift off one by one to the communal system of their village. They take pride in going back to do things *vaka viti,* the traditional Fijian way. I saw the former homes of several who were attempting peasant farming, built half a mile from their village in an effort to free themselves from the idea of the communal system. The houses had been abandoned, however, for the occupants had moved back among their kinsfolk.

Some chiefs have complained that lack of money for investment is a discouragement to Fijians to develop their lands commercially. This is true in some cases, but in a village receiving several hundred pounds a year as rent for native land, decrepit in appearance, it is hard to believe that commercial sugar cane production is being held up for lack of money to buy capital equipment (55, 17). Natives assert the need for machinery, which they could buy with the rent from their lands. "If there were greater diligence and less indolence the cry for capital would ring more true" (16, 42). There is little confidence that if actual cash were given, say a loan from the Fijian Development Fund, it would be spent on the alleged need (55, 69). It must be stated that there is doubt about the collateral of loans because of the unavailability of *mataqali* land as security (55, 66). An Indian with a lease can use his land as guarantee for repayment of a loan, whereas this is not possible for Fijians whose land is inalienable and held communally.

Fijians have no sense of a money economy, for the discipline of a monetary world has never been learned. They are not only uninterested in western business methods, but they are indifferent toward learning anything about them. A native has no incentive to acquire money except to satisfy the desire for a particular luxury—a new *sulu,* a lamp, kerosene, or a contribution to his church. If he hasn't any such objective, he will let the surplus of his garden rot, rather than trouble to take it to market (57, 83). Natives on sugar cane farms often sell fertilizer supplied by the CSR to the Indians at half its market price, using the cash to satisfy immediate wants (55, 3). A Fijian buys articles at more than their actual value if he suddenly desires them; he sells them at less if he needs cash. He knows that his basic maintenance is assured by the village, and so can afford to be reckless with whatever money or possessions he has.

It is generally alleged that the factor which most hinders the progress of Fijians is their traditional system of *kere kere*. "Begging," or in their way of thinking "sharing" with kinsfolk is a custom from which they seem unable to free themselves. An attribute "which was formerly the pivot of native society, now wars unceasingly against the mercantile progress of the people" (51, 80). To say "no" to a request for something which he has, seems almost impossible for a Fijian. The custom militates strongly against commercial farming, for, when he sells his sugar cane to the mill, his friends come to "borrow" money. If a man has a good crop of taro or yams, his neighbors will soon command the surplus. At the gold mines on pay day, relatives of the workers flock there to sponge. Those with money accede to *kere kere* as the only way known to them of fulfilling their duty to their kinsfolk and villages. "A young man returning to his village after a year's work on a plantation, may be the proud possessor of a wrist watch, a new box, a gray shirt, or a well-tailored *sulu;* but it is probable that before a week is out, the watch will be on another's wrist, the box in a friend's house, and the clothes either borrowed or appropriated by his relations" (27, 126). A chief said to me, "I started a business and got a manager, but he used to give away the goods on credit, and never was paid for them. Soon our debts were so big that we could not get any wholesale house to give us credit. Our old custom of sharing everything is still strong within us."

Before a Fijian storekeeper realizes it, he has disposed of half his goods by *kere kere*. A village store belongs to everyone (53, 159).

The advantages of *kere kere* in traditional Fijian society are often disregarded or overlooked by western observers. As already implied, if a man were incapacitated for work by age or blindness, or unable to take care of himself because of sickness or other misfortune, the custom enabled him to be maintained and looked after by his kinsfolk in the community. As one of them, he was entitled to have the benefits of this observance and was provided with all the necessities of life (27, 127). It was first and foremost a form of social security, since by it a man's kin was bound to see him through material misfortune. It gave added value to kinship ties and contributed to social solidarity; it helped to spread consumption of goods; "politically it prevented the accumulation of wealth from becoming a threat to the hierarchy. It was thus both a social control and, because of the strong element of reciprocity, itself subject to social controls" (55, 24).

The traditional *kere kere* system is very much abused today. When the native is free to indulge in laziness, without fear of the ancient punishments, he begs from his neighbor to gratify his own indolence. "It has become a unilateral practice by inconsiderate beggars whose conduct is little short of covetousness" (51, 46). There is a tendency for the idle to live at the expense of an industrious minority (57, 83). Public opinion still prevents the richer native from refusing what is asked of him, though he knows that the recipient of his generosity is too idle and thriftless to be in a position to return the equivalent. Natives who deny the importunitities of their friends are made victims of an organized boycott which deters others from following their example. In one case a poultry farmer refused an inordinately high levy for flood repair. In retaliation the village billeted relays of his kin on him "till the last chicken had gone to pot" (55, 91). A native, therefore, has no incentive to be industrious, knowing that whatever he accumulates will soon be pre-empted by idle relatives.

Among other factors holding back the indigenous population and preventing economic and social progress is the attitude of the chiefs. They are not enthusiastic about independent farming and indeed merely tolerate it (16, 33). If that method of agriculture becomes general, they foresee the disappearance of communal tribute or service on behalf of the village *lala,* and they don't know of anything to take its place. The more successful the peasant farmer *(galala),* the less will become their authority and prestige. This attitude of those who are still regarded by the rank and file of the native population as their leaders is important and very discouraging to the commoners.

As part of the whole picture of native life today, we must realize that the Fijians are socially and psychologically demoralized. Work in the villages is falling more and more heavily on the older people, as young men move out to try to find jobs elsewhere. Standards of housing have deteriorated, and many native structures in the vicinity of urban centers are dilapidated. In villages near Suva, in 1960, I observed the worn, ragged thatch of roofs and walls, and other signs of neglect and decay. Even in an outlying village, where the home of one of my friends, a high chief, is located, the thatch needed repair, and the Methodist Church required renovation. For a number years, the government has encouraged the Fijians to build houses with iron roofs, which last much longer than the grass-covered structures. However, 63 per cent of the native houses in the Colony are constructed of the traditional materials (20, 51). Nearly all the Europeans in the colony have houses with galvanized iron roofs, a common type of building for them in the tropics; the same holds true in Fiji for the part-Europeans. The Indians who live in this form of structure considerably outnumber the Fijians. Details of the ethnic groups with thatch and iron roofs are given in Table 17 in the appendix.

There is a drift of the indigenous people to the towns on Viti Levu and Vanua Levu, in part because of expected opportunities for unskilled jobs, and also because of the decline of the traditional village system. The communal system seems destined not to survive much longer, at least not without considerable modifications. The census of 1956 showed 24.5 per cent of the Fijians absent from their provinces, which indicates the same ratio of absences from villages. This means that a quarter of those away paid the commutation rate to be relieved of the traditional village duties and, therefore, had more or less permanently contracted out of the village system (55, 70). A young man from the Lau Islands said to me in Suva, "The Lau Islands are not modern like Viti Levu; that's why I came over here to get a job. I pay my pound and my taxes to Lau. The villages in my islands are still old Fiji;" he added, "very few iron roofs." A Fijian working at Nadi Air Port told me that he pays one pound a year to his province in lieu of communal work on trails and roads, and about six pounds in rates and school taxes.

People coming from the country live on kinsmen already settled in the towns which leads to serious overcrowding (55, 75). Since the families generally stay behind, there are just as many houses needed in the villages, although there are fewer men to build them. In more densely populated areas, local supplies of thatching materials, bamboo, and other timber are now more difficult to obtain.

Traditional village festivals inland from towns are celebrated by the natives even with more zeal than formerly, in part to compensate for the loss of prestige in their own archipelago and for the vanity of display. Furthermore, the introduction of fresh beef and canned foods of various kinds have added much to the native menu. Great feasts constitute a serious drain on the native economy. The ordinary activities of a village cease for two or three days while the normal working force, together, with the population in general, carry on the customary festivities which accompany births, marriages and deaths. The expense of these activities is often a crushing burden (55, 25). In a village of few livestock during one year, eight cattle were slaughtered for funeral feasts; and building six new houses accounted for nine (55, 26). Large amounts of canned fish are also consumed at the celebrations.

A government officer inspecting the accounts of provincial funds reported outstanding debts for ceremonial occasions long since past. He went on to state that when the presentation of food and material goods *(yau)* took place in olden times, this truly represented the fruits of the earth and the labors of those making the gifts, for there was no "price" of the ceremony in money terms; but that now the fat pig has to be purchased, and the lorries and other vehicles bringing those who perform the ceremonies have to be hired, at no little expense. The debts also included those for new school buildings not promptly paid off at the time when these were built (10, 12).

Many of the social functions of the Fijians are part of their church activities. They are overwhelmingly Christian, due to the activities of missionaries from the early 1830's down to the present. More than 99 per cent of them belong to some Christian denomination, as do a similar proportion of Rotumans and other Pacific islanders in the colony. Eighty-five per cent of the Fijians are Wesleyan Methodists. On the other hand, less than three per cent of the Indians are Christians; 81 per cent of them are Hindus (Table 18 in the appendix).

Christianity, however, is in part a veneer over native animism. The Fijian has a vague but strong belief in spiritual beings; he lives in great fear of evil spirits; he believes that isolated and uninhabited spots on his island are haunted. "Fiji literally swarms with miscellaneous spirits. The tops of the hills, the gloom of the forests, the running streams and waterfalls, stones, capes, bays, and the ocean are crowded with them" (25, 31). The primitive Fijian was essentially an animist. He believed in a soul or a personality separate from living man. Everyone thought a human being would live beyond the grave. The native was also a firm believer in ghosts or the appearance of the separate personality after death (37, 260). Some of these tenets of his faith made it easy for him to take over the new religion because of the resemblance.

Their church affiliations, however, and the attachment to their new religion, which can be observed in Centenary Church in Suva, and in the other churches throughout the islands, do little to counteract the disappointment and frustration which the indigenous people feel at the gradual disappearance of their traditional way of life, and the loosening of their old village ties. The unhappy natives have accepted an attitude of fatalism (55, 36). Their feelings have resulted in slackness and casualness; they are aware of their lack of will power to stand out against the demands of kinsfolk, and to follow a recognizably desirable course of conduct; they know that they are careless and frivolous spenders, and that they throw away future gains for an immediate gratification; they acknowledge that they want to impress—especially the Indians—by conspicuous expenditures.

The Fijian is vain. In the old days he loved to parade his valor to attract public attention. At times he was exceptionally brave on the battlefield hoping to enjoy the prestige of a chief for a while after his return. He would submit to a painful ceremony to enjoy prestige and appreciation (34, 70). He loves display and showing off. Not long ago, a man drove a new tractor to church on Sunday (55, 92).

Had the Fijians remained isolated from Europeans, Indians, and other aliens, their society would, undoubtedly, have remained stationary for centuries; there would have been no stimulus to break down the law of custom. In thinking over the circumstances of the native population since Europeans first came to their islands, we cannot but recall Rousseau's doctrine of primitivism, which held that mankind could be noble and happy only in a primitive society. Certainly the Fijian chiefs at this moment advocate Rousseau's belief in the right of a country or state to live its own life free from outward interference, and to shape its destinies according to its own will (59). The philosopher's idea that "property" is the cause of the injustice of man's social existence would justify *kere kere*. His affirmation of the superiority of "primitive" people to civilized man, fashionable especially after his death, can be maintained by the Fijians today.

We have reserved for later discussion one other factor which has contributed to the plight of the indigenous people, namely, the administration of the archipelago. But before the government is discussed, it is necessary to go into details of the Indian population in the islands.

PART III

The Indians

CHAPTER 4

Origin and Background of the Indians

THE INDIAN emigrants were recruited under the supervision of the government of India. When an immigrant finished his five years service under indenture, and, in addition, any extension of time imposed by a court, he received a certificate of industrial residence to become a "free man." He could then pay his way back to India if he wished. But the free man could reindenture for five years, or work for an employer as a free laborer, take up a craft or trade, or settle on a plot of land for the same length of time. After the additional term, that is after 10 years residence in the colony, he had the privilege of being repatriated at the expense of the government of Fiji. At least 40 women were recruited for every 100 men (66, 136).

The Indians who emigrated to Fiji came from various parts of the subcontinent. The majority were northerners from the extensive plains of what were formerly called "The United Provinces" (now Uttar Pradesh); most of them from the eastern part, and from Bihar Province (40, 2). For the first decade or so following 1879, emigration was slow, but it gathered momentum during the '90's, until by 1896 the Indian population in Fiji numbered some 10,000. At the beginning of the new century, immigration to the colony increased still further, for labor was in demand because of the expansion of the sugar industry. There was a constant stream of immigrants, and by 1912, Indians in Fiji numbered 50,000 (27, 138).

The agricultural people who came during the early part of the immigration were followed at intervals in later years by an entirely different type. Among them were Gujeratis from what was then the Bombay Presidency—most of them from a district near Surat in the north; they came at their own expense. There followed close friends and relatives. All of them emigrated because they could earn a better living in Fiji than in Gujerat. They were traders, tailors, shoemakers, barbers, laundrymen and jewelers (40, 1, 3).

Following the Gujeratis came people from the Punjab who were peasant farmers and dairymen; the majority were Sikhs from Ludhiana and Jullunder, who had heard of the promising agricultural prospects in the colony. In the latter years of the importation of labor, southern Indians, darker skinned, came from the then Madras Presidency. A small number originated in the independent state of Nepal, some of whom formed a colony near Sigatoka on Viti Levu (40, 2, 3). Indian women of the agricultural and laboring classes were also induced to emigrate (9, 195).

The Indians talked very different languages. Those from the United Provinces and Bihar spoke Hindi and Bihari. Gujerati, a closely related language in a similar script, was spoken by those from the Bombay Presidency; the people from Madras used Tamil, Telugu, or other Dravidian languages. Table 19 (Appendix) gives the languages spoken by the Indians in Fiji.

The Indians represented different religions. The great majority were Hindus, of two sects: *Sanatan Dharmis* and *Arya Samajis* (40, 6). The Sikhs, from the Punjab, were those of a militant sect which arose within Hinduism in India during a period of Reformation. About 10 per cent of the arrivals were predominantly Sunni Muslims, who spoke Urdu (40, 10).

In India the Hindus were subject to a rigid caste system which determined their occupations, their social positions, and duties within the community. Rules regulated marriage, stipulated preferred occupations and held certain foods to be impure. Regulations prescribed the conditions and degree of social intercourse permitted between the several castes. Caste was an all-pervading principle of attraction and repulsion, which entered into and shaped every relationship of life.

Caste was bound up with religion, the observances of which were enforced by the authority of the priests. It was a polytheistic pantheism in which Brahma was regarded as the one and original *cause*. Several important deities were worshipped as were many of lesser importance. Orthodox Brahmanism had to associate itself with all manner of gross superstitious and to us, Westerners, repulsive practices. Special times of year were set apart for different religious observances. Muslims lived entirely apart from Hindus, regarded them with animosity, and held their own religious ceremonies and observances. The backgrounds of Hinduism and Mohammedanism, from which the Indians came to Fiji, were made up of social and religious fabrics very different from those of the Fijians.

The early arrivals came from a hard-working agricultural background; they were peasant farmers, many of them just eking out a living. In the United Provinces, the practice was for a landlord to let his land to tenants, while he himself lived on the rents they paid, taking no part in cultivation. The tenants worked small holdings of four or five acres, each assisted by his family. Any capital which could be invested in their farms was that which their own small means and slender credit could supply. Everywhere agriculture was in the hands of "small masters," working independently on their own account. There was great competition in a never-ending struggle for land among the cultivators; if they were tenants they were driven by the force of competition to pay rack rents; if proprietors, their insatiable land hunger brought them to the door of the money-lender (42, 38 ff.). In the eastern part of the United Provinces, landlords owned 82 per cent of the village land (60, 111).

In the United Provinces in general, "absolute poverty" was proverbial. Land was fragmented, and holdings uneconomical. A farmer scratched the ground with a plow— a rough piece of wood sharpened at one end, a handle at the other, and a rough-cut branch for a shaft; the implement was drawn by an ox. In his various agricultural operations, the peasant used the techniques of the Middle Ages. Rents were exorbitant and landlords had the power to eject tenants at will (44, 142 ff.).

Land, greatly in demand, was the main investment of the lower classes, and various rights of tenancy and subtenancy were sold at good prices. The indebtedness of the Indian farmer is indicated by the fact that in some districts more than half of the farmers had to borrow their seed-grain (54, 48 ff.). There was "desperate over-pressure

14. INDIAN FARMERS. Settlement and colonization by the Indians rather than mere temporary labor engagements was encouraged. It was stated in a dispatch to India in 1875, "Indian settlers who have completed the terms of service . . . will be in all respects free men, with privileges no whit inferior to those of any other class of Her Majesty's subjects resident in the Colonies."

on agriculture" and "paralyzing burdens of exploitation" were placed on the peasantry (28, 37, 73).

The monsoon climate was a hazard for farmers. In India on the Ganges Plain, a hot, wet summer is often followed by a mild winter and a very hot, dry, spring. In April and May, a scorching wind blows from the western desert, laden with dust; occasionally such storms lower visibility to 100 yards. The rains generally come with the south and southwest monsoons, between June 1 and September 30. In some years they are appreciably less than in others. Indeed farmers on the sub-continent are slaves of variation in rainfall. They mix sorghum, wheat, and other grains of different resistance to drought, so that they may get at least some return from the very dry soil, and thus escape famine. Indian agriculture supports a population which is pressing so closely on its resources that every adverse circumstance pushes the greater part of the cultivators below the level of subsistence. India is a "desperately struggling" country where the miseries of the wretched agriculturists are unending (62, 4, 10).

The Indians lived in village communities which provided most of their own needs in food, clothing, and shelter. Houses were built of mud, bamboo, and thatching grass; agricultural implements were primitive, and many people did not eat more than once a day. Lacking wood and coal they used dried cowdung for fuel. Malnutrition was the chief cause of disease (32, 124).

The Indians who came to Fiji from the Punjab were also peasant farmers. Their principal crops were wheat and sugar cane, both of which were cash crops, that is they could be sold for money instead of being consumed or bartered. They also grew maize, rice, millet, cotton, and various other crops, and kept cattle for plowing and for their milk. Regularly industrious, "there was never a time when there was no work to be done" (63, 249). They yearned for land, which was the most valuable property passing from father to son.

The Gujeratis in their homeland were the local shop-keepers and also moneylenders. They sold things on credit higher than the price at which they would be given for cash. Once a farmer got into the clutches of a money lender, he found it difficult to free himself. He had to depend for the disposal of his crops on the same money lender, and thus he was doubly hit both in his selling and in his buying transactions. "The money lender was all supreme" (43, 80). Those who owned farms in fee simple, mortgaged their land to money lenders who often fore-closed (60, 108).

Only a small proportion of the immigrants re-engaged for plantation labor on the expiration of their original indenture; they preferred to work in other ways, especially to obtain land and cultivate it, and to make money gener-ally as "free men" (7). On December 31, 1907, the number of Indian residents in the colony was estimated at 30,920, of whom 11,689 were under indenture on the sugar cane plantations; the remainder were free settlers. During that year, many of them rented holdings from the natives in isolated localities; others leased land directly from the government. Some found work as domestic servants or laborers in the towns and on public works, while a few took to retail trading; a considerable number settled down as cattle breeders. At the end of that year the Indians operated 17,204 acres on their own. The chief crops they grew were sugar cane, 5,586 acres, which they supplied to neighboring mills, and rice, 9,347 acres. In 1909, at the end of their period of indenture, about 10 per cent re-engaged themselves on sugar estates for periods of one to three years. The great majority merged themselves in work among the general population of the colony (8, 85 ff.). During five years, 1904 to 1909, 8,000 Indians came under indenture, while 2,200 returned to India (8, 85 ff.).

Settlement and colonization by the Indians rather than mere temporary labor engagements were encouraged (9, 194). It was recommended that the colony should provide grants of land on easy terms to attract the immigrants to remain (8, 8). It was stated in a dispatch to India in 1875, "Indian settlers who have completed the terms of service to which they agreed as the return for the expense of bringing them to the Colonies, will be in all respects free men, with privileges no whit inferior to those of any other class of Her Majesty's subjects resident in the Colonies" (9, 195). It was held in Fiji that the colony gained by the addition to its population of a large body of hard-working and thrifty people from Asia. The Administration recognized their value as permanent settlers, and was willing to concede them the enjoyment of equal civil rights (8, 87).

The organized immigration of Indians to Fiji continued until 1917, when the Government of India put a stop to it. During the entire period from 1879 to 1916, a total of 62,837 were introduced under indenture. Of these, 24,655 exercised their right to repatriation; others went back later (27, 138). As the years went on, important changes in the nature and the attitude of that part of the population of the colony took place. Of 40,286 Indians in Fiji numbered in the census of 1911, some 27 per cent had been born in the islands. The remaining 73 per cent for the most part regarded themselves as living in a foreign country. In 1936, however, the picture was very different; at that time, of 85,002 Indians in the archipelago, approximately 72 per cent were locally born. In 1946 of a total of 120,043, 85 per cent were born in Fiji. Nearly all the remaining 15 per cent had been residents in the Colony for more than ten years. That census showed that the Indian population of the archipelago had surpassed that of the Fijian. The number of Indians overtook and passed the number of Fijians between 1940 and 1946, due to the absence of native men, fewer marriages, and consequent falling off in Fijian births. During those years of World War II, some 7,700 Fijians served voluntarily with the armed forces of Great Britain, about 3,000 of whom were abroad for various periods. The figures for the Indians were 264 volunteers, of whom one went abroad (20a). In 1956, the great majority of Indian infants, young people, and those of middle age were born in the colony. Most of those over 60 were born in India and Pakistan (Table 20).

The following table gives the growth in Indian population in Fiji from 1901 to 1961 (16, 10)

TABLE 6
GROWTH OF INDIAN POPULATION IN FIJI

YEAR	NUMBER	YEAR	NUMBER
1901	17,105	1946	120,414
1911	40,286	1956	169,403
1921	60,634	1958	178,090
1936	85,002	1961	206,819

The vast majority of Indians in Fiji today are Fiji-born descendants of immigrants introduced from India. They look upon Fiji as the land of their adoption. They are an integral part of the local population, permanently settled in the colony. They have inherited from the culture of their fathers and grandfathers an unusual capacity for hard work and endurance, frugal habits, capable organization of business, and great perseverance. Their frugality and industry stem from the rigorous social and economic environment of the Asian subcontinent. They have flourished exceedingly in the fertile soil to which they were transplanted.

CHAPTER 5

Indian Initiative and Energy

THE INDIANS have contributed enormously to the economic development of Viti Levu and Vanua Levu, by far the two larger and more important islands of the Fijian archipelago, the natural resources of which have been turned to account mainly by the energy and industry of the colonists; the soil has been made to yield abundant quantities of sugar cane, rice, and other products. The professional ability and business acumen of the better educated of these people from India have been of signal value socially, and in trade and commerce.

Tenant Farmers

Indians are pre-eminently the sugar cane farmers of Fiji, for its cultivation is well understood by them. The growing season, from planting to harvesting, is generally from 14 to 18 months, and a ratoon crop is obtained. When the first crop has been harvested, the leaves and other "trash" are burned to clear the field and to destroy insect pests. The roots soon put forth new shoots to grow into a second

95

crop. When that matures and is harvested, the roots and trash are plowed into the soil to provide humus. Beans and other legumes are grown as rotation crops to be worked into the soil, and after a period of fallow, the field is planted again in sugar cane. Under this regime, at any given time, a quarter of the land is in "plant" cane, a similar area in a ratoon crop, a quarter is under a legume, and the remainder fallow. On rich land, the stages are reduced, so that more land is under crop. At Lautoka, on CSR land, I noted adjacent farms of 10 acres, each laid out in four sections of two and a half acres, used as follows: plant crop, ratoon, fallow, Mauritius beans.

	A	B	C	D
Farm 1	Plant crop	Plant crop	Plant crop	Plant crop
„ 2	Ratoon	Ratoon	Ratoon	Ratoon
„ 3	Fallow	Fallow	Fallow	Fallow
„ 4	Mauritius beans	Mauritius beans	Mauritius beans	Mauritius beans

By this arrangement in adjoining sections, the four divisions are ready to be worked, or harvested conveniently by machinery at the same time. It also facilitates laying railway tracks to haul cane to the mills.

The Indian farmhouse is generally a one-story galvanized iron or frame building on posts about two feet above the ground. It is very small, about 24 feet each way, has wooden frames with hinges at the top for windows, which open towards the interior of the house; there is no chimney. Consisting of two or three rooms, and no furniture except beds, there are mats on the floor to sit on. Women cook *roti,* bread made from wheat flour fried in *ghee* (rendered butter), and curried rice, in a pan on two or three iron bars across a brick fireplace outside; in rainy weather on a little stove inside. Some have chicken coops at the back,

15. INDIAN FARMERS LOADING SUGAR CANE. Great increases in world production of this commodity has caused an imposition of a quota on Fijian export of sugar. This one-crop economy handicaps the agricultural development of the archipelago to its fullest extent.

16. FIJIAN-TYPE HOUSE OF INDIAN FARMERS. An Indian generally works on his farm along with his wife and children helping in the fields to hoe and weed. Sometimes a father or a brother lives with him and does a share of the work.

and not far away, several goats. Oxen are usually tethered under a mango or wild plum tree near the house; a plow and a harrow stand in the open near the cane field.

An Indian generally works his farm along with his wife and children helping in the fields to hoe and weed. Sometimes a father or a brother lives with him and does a share of the work. An overseer of the CSR Company keeps strict supervision over agricultural operations.

Oxen are commonly used for draft animals, for they are strong and cheap to feed. They eat grass gleaned from uncultivated slopes near sugar cane land, from road sides, and from wasteland or swamps; farmers have small plots of "para" grass for fodder. Zebu cattle have been bred with European stock to better adapt the cross to the local climate, and to combine the good qualities of both.

Indians work hard. Men normally rise about daybreak, and go to work for two or three hours before eating a small breakfast. Wives take lunches out to the fields for their husbands. I met the men trudging home at dusk after a long, hard day. During school vacations, whole families work together, even small children doing what they can. They live mostly in houses on or very near their farms, and in scattered locations till them independently of each other, plowing with oxen and fertilizing when necessary. Many have their own machinery and work animals, and some have tractors. They generally cut sugar cane co-operatively, neighbor helping neighbor.

About half of the Indian cultivators are tenants of the sugar cane company, working farms of 10 to 12 acres. The company furnishes them fertilizer, and the use of farm machinery on credit, and makes cash advances at a low rate of interest. Accounts are settled when the cane has been ground in the mill. The mills close for several months in January, the commencement of the rainy season, for then the sugar content of the cane begins to be low.

All the growers are obliged to follow the advice and directions of agricultural specialists regarding planting and the use of the land, including the Indian cane farmers who cultivate land leased from the Fijians. If they neglect to follow the advice of the company's officers, and the quality of the cane suffers, the CSR may refuse (in extreme cases) to take it, and the crop is left on their hands (27, 168). The Colonial Sugar Refining Company has taught the Indians modern agriculture: plant breeding, disease control, how to experiment with fertilizers, the use of legumes, and other aspects of growing sugar cane.

The 9,500 sugar-cane farms in the colony are nearly all Indian-leased or Indian-owned, and are "sufficiently small to be operated, on the average, by less than two adult males, even in the cane cutting and crushing season" (20, 49). Seventy-five per cent of Indian males on the land earn a living in the sugar industry, and are responsible for 90 per cent of the production (16, 40). Most of the land in the Colony best suited to growing cane and near to the sugar mills has been leased by them. The following table shows the tons of cane crushed and the weight grown by Indians and Fijians.

TABLE 7
SUGAR CANE GROWN
BY INDIANS AND FIJIANS

YEAR	TONS OF CANE CRUSHED	TONS GROWN BY INDIANS	TONS GROWN BY FIJIANS
1948	943,600	911,927	31,673
1959	2,447,251	283,005 (of sugar)	no data—"Fijian share of acreage and output has never exceeded about five per cent" (55, 3)

17. INDIAN QUARTER IN TAORAK, SUVA. It is in the cane areas that
the majority of the Indian people are settled. Market towns have
grown up at all the main sugar centers; they comprise especially
the stores and shops of Indian traders and craftsmen engaged in
supplying the needs of the cane growers.

18. INDIAN HOMES IN SUVA. The Indians have advanced far beyond the economic and social status of their relatives on the subcontinent. Many have acquired Western culture: live in European-style houses, drive automobiles, look at British and American movies, and have radios in their homes.

It is in the cane areas that the majority of the Indian people are settled. Market towns have grown up at all the main sugar centers; they comprise especially the stores and shops of Indian traders and craftsmen engaged in supplying the needs of cane growers. Indian rice farmers and millers, and those who are mixed farmers take up land as far as they can near the market towns (27, 99). The map showing the distribution of the Indian population (Fig. 19) also indicates in general the location of the sugar-producing areas on Viti Levu and Vanua Levu. The four "sugar towns," closely associated with the mills of the CSR, have a large population of Indians. Lautoka had a total number of 7,420 people in 1956 of whom approximately 4,000 were Indians; Ba had 2,007 out of a total of 2,381. Both these are on the northwest side of Viti Levu. Labasa in northeast Vanua Levu with some 2,200 people had also a large majority of Indians. Nausori in southeast Viti Levu had 860 out of 1,105, but it has lost a considerable number of people since the sugar mill there closed down, in 1959.

The exports of sugar from Fiji and their value (Table 21) indicate the importance of this crop to the economy of these small islands in the mid-Pacific. During the last six or seven years they have increased markedly to bring significant wealth to the archipelago, and large dividends to the Colonial Sugar Refining Company. Since 1946, including that year, the amount sent out has reached over 100,000 tons annually, gradually increasing until it is now more than 200,000 tons, valued at over £8 million.

The ethnic distribution of crops in the Colony (Table 23) shows the importance of the contribution of the Indians to this aspect of its wealth. In 1958 they operated 118,184 acres out of a total of 128,863 used for that crop. The share of the Fijians was only 8,448 acres. Furthermore,

8,791 Indians were in proprietary, managerial, and executive positions in the sugar industry, and other Indian workers in it totalled 8,047 (Table 22). The Fijian representation in the first category was 479, and in the second 782. Other ethnic groups engaged in growing sugar cane and processing it were of minimal importance.

The share of crops of the various ethnic groups also indicates the aptitude of the Indians for growing rice, a crop which requires hard work. They use 30,150 acres for it out of a total of 31,200 (Table 23). The Fijian portion is only 400 acres, the same amount as for the Chinese and all others. The Fijians excel in growing coconuts and bananas —tree crops, which require little cultivation. They operate half the area of land in the islands used for coconuts and nearly all the area used for bananas. In raising native crops (taro, cassava, yams, and others), they far surpass the acreage of the Indians.

The distribution of land ownership in the archipelago (Table 24) indicates the large area of land owned in freehold by Europeans, including that of the Colonial Sugar Refining Company which has title to some 75,000 acres, 1.7 per cent of the total area of the Colony. Other Europeans and part-Europeans, who make up four per cent of the population, own 246,242 acres, 5.5 per cent of the area of the islands. The Indians come next with some 75,830 acres, 1.7 per cent approximately of the whole. The Fijians have registered titles to only 7,532 acres or 0.2 per cent. However, by native customary tenure, they hold 3,776,000 acres in traditional tribal ownership, 83.6 per cent of the total area. Although the Indians own only 1.7 per cent of the land of the Colony, they occupy and farm a much larger proportion of the total cultivatable acreage. This includes a considerable amount of the better and more fertile lands, where the most remunerative crop, sugar cane is grown. They have leased land in widely scattered areas of Viti Levu and Vanua Levu, by far the larger part of it from Fijians (Table 8). The next important lessor is the Colonial Sugar Refining Company. They have also rented thousands of acres from the government and from Europeans.

The following table indicates the approximate acreage leased to Indians (16, 19).

TABLE 8

LAND LEASED TO INDIANS (in acres)

	IN THE CANE BELTS	ELSE-WHERE	TOTAL LEASED
By Fijians	150,000	80,000	230,000
By the Crown (freehold)	5,000	15,000	20,000
By the Crown (Schedule A and B lands)	2,000	18,000	20,000
By the Colonial Sugar Refining Co.	50,000	—	50,000
By other freeholders	15,000	15,000	30,000
TOTALS	222,000	128,000	350,000

Rice is the crop second in importance to Indian farmers, some of whom raise it in addition to sugar cane. It is planted in swampy areas on the plains of Lekutu, Sarawaqa, and Dreketi; it is also grown south of Naduri, west of Tabia, in the Bucaisau Valley (27, 250), and in the delta land of the Rewa River. The grain is sown in December in seed beds, and transplanted in January for a three to four months growing period; it is cut with a sickle in March or April. One acre supplies a family with cereal food for a year.

Wet land paddy necessitates continuous manual work,

endured by the Indians but shunned by Fijians. The seedlings have to be taken from the seed beds, and transplanted in fields which must get the right amount of water. Farmers try to have all transplanting done while the rainfall is favorable. Men, women, and children turn out for that backbreaking work, standing up to their knees in the slushy mud. It is necessary to weed between the rows of stalks and between the growing plants—a long, dull chore. The crop is harvested just when it is ripe, and may not be left long to burn in the sun (39, 41).

A considerable number of Indians engage in diversified agriculture. They raise *yaqona,* European vegetables for the market in Suva, and crops for their own subsistence. Many of them keep cattle, especially for their milk from which they make *ghee;* cattle are always seen wherever there is an Indian population. I visited the Dip Singh farm which is representative of some of the larger and more successful Indian holdings. Dip Singh belongs to a strict Hindu sect, members of which will not eat any meat at all. He will not raise cattle for beef, nor poultry to kill. Singh cannot speak a word of English, and since three of us, including the Director of Agriculture for the colony, accepted an invitation to lunch, the meal was for the most part in silence. The third member of our party, an Indian Agricultural Assistant, told us what the dishes were: *bara,* black grain with onions fried in *ghee; sehna,* taro leaves boiled for vegetables; *puri,* made from wheat middlings; *dahl* soup; *achar,* a condiment made from chili peppers and mangoes; cucumber and radish salad; coreander chutney, and boiled rice.

Dip Singh has 200 acres of land in freehold, 100 of which are leased to other farmers. When we visited him, he had 20 acres in bananas, 26 in rice, half an acre each of pota-

20. INDIAN FARMER IN PASSION FRUIT ORCHARD. Almost all of the early immigrants from India were farmers in their homeland, but only a small proportion of this group re-engaged for plantation labor on the expiration of their original indenture, preferring to work in other ways to obtain land and to generally make money as "free men."

21. INDIAN FARMS IN SIGATOKA. Although Indian farmers are "in clover" in Fiji, there is a growing dissatisfaction among them, which has become stronger during the last two or three decades. Their most serious grievance is the inability to obtain sufficient land for further settlement and cultivation.

toes and pumpkins, and a few small patches of watermelons and ginger. Young coffee trees, of the *robusta* variety, were shaded by banana plants. He kept 18 milk cows which he grazed on 25 acres of "para" grass, and what they could browse on in another area of his farm. He made *ghee* and sold milk in the local Nausori market.

The Indians in Fiji are active in many other occupations besides farming. Some of them have gone abroad for a higher education, and have returned from universities overseas as qualified lawyers, physicians, and dentists. Of 56 attorneys in the colony, 38 are Indians. I noted four applications from Indians to practice before the Supreme Court as barristers and solicitors, posted outside the door of the court room in the Government Building in Suva.

The following table shows the lawyers, doctors, and dentists in Fiji in 1958 (16, 12).

TABLE 9

LAWYERS, DOCTORS, AND DENTISTS*

PROFES-SIONS	INDIANS	FIJIANS	EURO-PEANS	PART-EURO-PEANS	CHINESE	TOTAL
Lawyers	38	—	17	1	—	56
Doctors	12	1	51	1	1	66
Dentists	8	1	6	—	—	15
TOTAL	58	2	74	2	1	137

Indian storekeepers do considerable retail business in both urban and rural settlements. They engage in importing, especially foodstuffs and cloth from the country of their origin. Some of them operate large concerns. I

---

* This table excludes 97 Fijian and 18 Indian Assistant Medical Officers trained at Suva Medical School, but not qualified by professional degrees in medicine from universities.

visited the Hari Company garment factory in Suva where 100 women are employed, and saw the headquarters of the Narain Construction Company, the largest building concern in Fiji. The energy of the colonists is indicated by the fact that from five villages close together near the mouth of the Rewa River, men go to work every morning in Suva. They leave their homes at seven o'clock, go down the Rewa on launches to Waimbokasi, where they get buses to arrive at their offices or other places of business in the city at eight-thirty.

The Indians have a near monopoly in road transport; most bus services are owned and operated by them. A considerable amount of marketing for Fijians is done by Indian truck-owners who make up their loads for the market by picking up small lots in the native villages. Fijians, however, predominate in water transport in the proportion of five to one. In commerce there are 3,000 Indians to 1,000 Fijians with an eight to one proportion of Indians in the top brackets (55, 48, 74).

Many Indians are wealthy. In 1960 an income of over £5,000 accrued to each of 42 people in the Colony of whom 16 were Indians; of the remainder, 21 were Europeans and five Chinese (4, 125). The net profits assessed for taxes in individual business and in partnerships in 1957 shows the relative importance of four ethnic groups.

The following table gives the figures (16, 11).

TABLE 10

NET PROFITS ASSESSED FOR TAXES, 1957

ETHNIC GROUP	NO. PERSONS ASSESSED	PER CENT OF TOTAL ASSESSED	NET PROFIT ASSESSED FIJIAN	PER CENT OF NET PROFIT ASSESSED
Indian	9,076	88.6	£3,582,301	76.8

Fijians and Others	134	1.4	41,815	0.9
European	634	6.2	696,201	14.9
Chinese	401	3.8	348,494	7.4
TOTAL	10,245	100.0	£4,668,811	100.0

The above figures include agriculture which, if it is excluded, drops the proportion of Fijians to the total number assessed from 1.4 per cent to 0.9 per cent, and the proportion of their net profit assessed from 0.9 per cent to 0.4 per cent. The handicap of the easy going nature of the Fijians, and the effects of their culture are indicated by the fact that in 1957, out of a total of some 3,000 individual or business partnerships assessed for tax, only 25 of them were Fijian (16, 12).

The distribution of income tax payments by ethnic groups in the archipelago indicates the relative importance of the Indians to the Fijians, and to other racial groups in the islands.

TABLE 11

DISTRIBUTION OF INCOME TAX PAYMENTS
BY ETHNIC GROUPS, 1958 (16, 145)

ETHNIC GROUP	NO. OF TAXPAYERS	TAX PAID (£ FIJIAN)	TAX PER HEAD (£ FIJIAN)
Indians	5,169	160,768	31.10
Fijians and Others	1,241	10,738	8.65
Europeans	4,510	336,871	74.69
Chinese	921	35,463	38.50
TOTAL	11,841	543,840	45.93

Many Indians in Fiji, especially in Suva, and Chinese, too, have acquired western culture. They live in European-style houses, eat European food as well as some of their traditional dishes. They drive automobiles, look at British and American movies, and have radios in their homes. Samabula, the Indian residence district in a suburb of Suva has streets well laid out, and attractive-looking homes, similar to those of Europeans in other parts of the city.

The Indians have advanced far beyond the economic and social status of their relatives on the subcontinent. "From humble and sometimes tragic beginnings in which they played the simple role of a labor force, Indians in Fiji have become a community with an important place in all aspects of the colony's life—business and professional men, experienced political leaders, craftsmen, mechanics, and farmers. . . Because of the restriction on ownership of land, capital has tended to be invested in towns in urban enterprises. But the farmer, nevertheless, remains the most important person in the Fiji Indian community, and a major factor in the Colony" (39, 12).

Sources of Indian Dissatisfaction

Although the Indians are "in clover" in Fiji, as an old-time resident of the islands stated, it must not be surmised that they are a happy and contented people. There is a growing dissatisfaction among them, which has become stronger and stronger during the last two or three decades. Their most serious grievance is the inability to obtain sufficent land for further settlement and cultivation. A very small proportion of them own farming land in fee simple; few have obtained freehold property.

Furthermore the Indians complain of the difficulty of

obtaining leases, the short terms on which leases are granted, and in many cases, their inability to renew them. They maintain that the principal hindrance to their further economic betterment is the insecurity of tenure of leased land. They maintain that they can, only with considerable difficulty, obtain even short-term leases from European freeholders or native land owners; and that when the term has expired, their renewal, particularly the renewal of native leases, presents many serious difficulties (41, 9). Furthermore they allege that on the expiration of many leases of native land, the areas are allowed to go out of cultivation, and that they become weed-infested and bush lands when they return to the native domain (41, 10). They argue that the Fijians have much land that they do not use and, they think, therefore, that it should be available to them. It is held that "many rents and premiums charged by some landlords are shocking" (18, 14). All improvements on land made during the period of a lease have to be turned over to the landlord without compensation on its expiration.

Sugar-cane farms of 10 to 12 acres can support at a fair living standard only one family. Even then the family will have to supplement its income away from the farm, or else engage in mixed farming. There are more Indians living on each farm than the single family originally envisaged (4, 187). At present "one-and-a-half" families live off the proceeds of one farm (18, 13). Members of the Burns Commission observed as many as two, three, and, in some instances, four separate families living on ten-acre holdings, although only the actual lessee or tenant is recognized as the farmer or operator (16, 40). However, the Indians in Fiji maintain the joint family system of India. Two or three sons in a family may bring wives to live under the family roof, literally, in adjoining houses, but subject to the dictates of the mother-in-law.

With regard to their social drawbacks in the Colony, the Indians complain of the lack of facilities for the education of their children. They maintain that funds available for education are not evenly or equitably distributed among all races and classes in the archipelago, and that institutions for their children comparable to those of other races are not provided. They argue that equal educational opportunities should be afforded for all children irrespective of race, religion, or the economic position of the parents (41, 21). There are only 153 Indian schools in the Colony as against 326 Fijian (55, 97). By far the greatest proportion of school-age children not attending school are Indian. According to the annual report on education for the year 1957, 14,038 Indian children of school age, six to 14 years, and 2,654 Fijian children, were not attending school the previous year (41, 22).

There has been also deep-rooted discontent among the Indians working on sugar cane plantations, due to a) "inadequate wages, and a feeling among workers that they are being exploited," and b) "discrimination and inequality of opportunity in the industry" (19, 28). Labor problems developed seriously during World War II, and have plagued the sugar industry since then. The whole economic system of the archipelago was gravely dislocated in 1943, when both Indian mill-workers and Indian sugar cane farmers went on strike, among other things for higher rates of pay. The action of the Indians against both the CSR and the government, at a very critical time of World War II, was bitterly resented by both the British and Fijians who were giving their full collaboration to Americans in the prosecution of the war. The situation caused serious loss to the public revenue and the community in general (4, 177).

Tension continued to develop and again became very serious in 1957 when three strikes occurred. Workers complained that wages paid by the CSR were inadequate for a fair standard of living. Fear and great discontent embittered industrial relations (19, 3).

Hard feelings continued and reached a crescendo in 1960. A ten-year contract of the cane farmers with the CSR ended on May 30 of that year, and they demanded better terms under a new pact. A deadlock between the company and the growers seemed disastrous because of prolonged delay in reaping ripe sugar cane. Pent up emotions became widespread. The main claim of the "Fiji Sugar Industry Employees' Association" for mill workers was a minimum rate of 2s.6d (35 cents) per hour for unskilled employees, and a system of job evaluation for those receiving a higher wage. "The Company's offer was to increase the minimum rate from 1s. 3.125d (17 cents) per hour to 1s. 4d (20 cents) per hour, combined with the condition that the weekly hours should be 48 in the crushing season, and 44 in the slack season" (19, 8).

The Governor of the Colony met with the leaders of Indian labor unions in an effort to settle the dispute. They were intransigent in regard to the terms of harvesting cane and renewal of work in the mills. Isolated sugar cane farmers were fearful of threats to burn their cane if they attempted to cut it, thereby contravening the orders of several unions to continue to strike. Threats of shooting them or members of their families, and of burning their homes and cane fields were made if they did not comply with the orders of the Indian leaders. It is easy to hide in a cane field and lay a fuse to set the field ablaze after the culprit has escaped from the vicinity. In spite of all precautions, fires reported to the police between June 1 and August 24, 1960, burned an estimated 12,289 tons of cane, valued at approximately £36,867. It was necessary to send troops of the regular army and territorial force to sugar-growing centers to quell riots. Police and special constables guarded cane fields, mills, water pipe-lines, and bridges (4, 178). Next to the crisis of 1943, this one was the most serious in the islands.

The situation in regard to land tenure as it affects the Indians in Fiji, their difficulty in leasing land, the labor troubles, and the general unrest of that racial group in the Colony, make problems of solution more pressing because of the marked increase in their population. As early as 1909 it was noted that their natural increase was considerable (8, 87). The significant growth since then has been due almost entirely to the excess of births over deaths. The birth rate has remained much the same for a number of years, but the death rate has been considerably reduced by taking advantage of modern medical knowledge and facilities. As already stated, the Indians in the islands now outnumber the Fijians.

The increase in Indian and Fijian population since 1881 shows the small proportion of Indians up to 1901, in that period a growth of from 0.46 per cent to 14.20 per cent (Table 25). The Fijians were 90 per cent of the total in the former year, and 78.6 per cent in the latter. From 1901 on, the Indians showed a steady percentage of increase at the expense of the natives, gradually acquiring, up to 1961, more than half the total population of the archipelago. In that year the Fijians were only 41.74 per cent of the total (Fig. 22).

One attribute which the Indians in Fiji possess in large

measure is aggressiveness. They continually demand more land and longer leases; they ask for loans for capital improvements; they persistently request more schools, and other social benefits. But most of all they insist on political changes which will give them more representation in the administrative affairs of the Colony. "The chief complaint of the Indian community is that the Colonial office has not in spirit or in letter, wittingly or otherwise, fulfilled its pledged word to accord parity of treatment to Indians with the other races in the Colony" (41, 11).

PART IV

Government

CHAPTER **6**

The Dual Government of Fiji

Fiji is a British Crown Colony. A governor, appointed by the Queen, to the Colonial office in London is responsible for its administration. He serves for a period of five years, and then goes on to another post. He is assisted by an Executive Council and a Legislative Council, in each of which Europeans, Fijians, and Indians are represented. The Governor and other senior officers are generally from Great Britain.

A Constitution laid down by Letters Patent of January 31, 1914, has been amended from time to time. A new Constitution in 1937, representing a compromise between nominative and elective principles, was designed to end long and embarrassing agitation carried on by the Indians for equality with other ethnic groups in the government of the Colony (45, 230).

Until very recently the Executive Council consisted of the Governor, the Colonial Secretary, the Attorney-General, the Financial Secretary, and six members nominated by the Governor; the latter included three unofficial members of the Legislative Council—a European, an Indian, and a

Fijian, each chosen by the representatives of his own race in the Legislative Council (4, 128). The other members were nominated at will by the Governor.

The Legislative Council consisted of the Governor and not more than sixteen nominated members: five nominated Fijian members chosen from a panel elected by the Council of Chiefs; three European elected members; two European nominated members; three Indian elected members; and two Indian nominated members; also a speaker who has always been a European. The majority of the members of the Legislative Council are nominees of the governor, or heads of his various departments.

The Europeans in the Colony, and the Chinese are directly governed by the Governor, the Executive Council, and the Legislative Council. The Indians are similarly governed, but in each of thirteen districts into which their population is divided, there is an Indian Advisory Committee which acts as a clearing-house for ideas in regard to Indian affairs. The Fijians in the archipelago have their own administration described below.

The Colony is divided into four administrative districts, each in the charge of a District Commissioner, who is assisted by one or more District officers. The districts are: Central, with headquarters at Nausori; Eastern, at Levuka; Northern, at Labasa; and Western, at Lautoka. There is a City Council at Suva, a Town Board at Lautoka, and five Township Boards, on all of which are representatives of the ethnic communities. The District Commissioner or District officers concerned are *ex officio* chairmen of the Thirteen Indian Advisory Councils; the councils have no administrative authority. All the other members are Indians (45, 231).

The Commissioners of the Divisions, and especially

their District officers, are those in closest touch with the rural people of the Colony including the Fijians. A considerable portion of their time is taken up with paperwork: writing reports on various problems and phases of life and living in their particular Districts and Divisions. The District officers send through their Commissioners to the Central Government in Suva accounts of labor and industrial relations in the sugar industry, measures taken to control the rhinoceros beetle, progress made on experimental plantings of cocoa and other crops. They report on communications, social services, and legal and judicial matters which have affected their bailiwicks. They send in accounts of Fijian affairs also, although, as already stated, the native population has a separate administration of its own. Their reports also include discussions of Indian affairs apart from their activities in the sugar industry.

District officers and their administrative assistants hear from the people themselves about domestic disputes, and their attention is drawn to those destitute who need relief. They are in close touch with Fijians who have been put in jail for non-payment of taxes. In various other ways they get to know the natives and their affairs well. For example, with regard to the native population, a District officer in his annual report stated, "The biggest achievement of the year was the repair of the community's old launch for which a new engine was bought from community funds. The launch, properly used, should help the community considerably in its sale of fish, etc., and in its transport problems generally" (10, 44). I was the guest of a District Officer on a visit to the Ringolds, a group of small islands of the archipelago northeast of Taveuni, where he was superintending the construction of a concrete tank for domestic water, installed for the benefit of

Fijians working there on a European copra plantation. The materials were supplied by the Department of Public Works. That Department and the others of the Central Administration are like those in any well-organized government.

The Public Works Department employs engineers, surveyors, architects, and others skilled in affairs of material benefit to the population of the archipelago. The administrative division of the Agricultural Department employs biochemists, entomologists, botanists, and others who specialize in various crops. It has a laboratories section, one in field agriculture, and a veterinary service; in addition there is also a Forestry Department. An Education Department and a Medical Department are two of the more important sections of the government. All of these serve equally the Fijians as well as the other ethnic groups in the Colony.

Side by side with the central government of Fiji is the Fijian Administration which has jurisdiction over all Fijians in the Colony. The ordinances and regulations which apply to them are made by the Fijian Affairs Board, the executive head of which is the Secretary for Fijian Affairs, who is responsible to the Governor for the whole native administration. These ordinances and regulations have the force of law, and are incorporated in a code called "The Fijian Affairs Regulations." Their first and most important purpose is to ensure the continuance of the native communal system, and the customs and observances traditionally associated with it. Furthermore, they provide a simple code of civil and criminal law easily comprehended both by the native magistrates and the people. They enable cases involving infringement of the regulations to be heard locally, and justice to be carried out speedily (4.

129). They are the organized political expression of the communal system, and provide the sanctions for its continuance. The regulations of the Fijian Affairs Board require the approval of the Legislative Council of the Colony which is generally given without question. That Board may provide for penalties up to a fine of £50, or a term of imprisonment not exceeding one year, or both (56, 570).

The burdens of the law are the demands of the communal system, given legal expression in the Fijian Regulations: making and maintaining roads, building and repairing houses, planting and cultivating food crops, supplying Fijian visitors with food, and so on. Most of the daily activities of nearly all rural Fijians are controlled by programs of work and other rules which are given legal sanction by these regulations (55, 22, 31). Two grades of Fijian courts deal with offenses against the regulations, by-laws, and orders. The lower or *tikina* court consists of one Fijian magistrate, and the higher or Provincial court consists of either three Fijian magistrates, or two Fijian magistrates and a district officer (56, 568).

The Fijian Affairs Board is composed of the Secretary for Fijian Affairs as chairman, the five Fijian members of the Legislative Council, a Legal Adviser, and a Financial Adviser (16, 30). The actions of the Board or any of its departments are not questioned or criticized in the Legislature of the Colony. The Board recommends the appointments in the echelon of native administrative officials who are then nominated by the governor, institutes regulations binding on the Fijians, and controls the provincial budgets (4, 131). It has its own treasury with its own financial and legal advisers divorced from the Central Government; it has also its own system of taxation.

The origin of the Fijian administration goes back to the

policy of the first governor of Fiji, who had to find some way of preventing the rapid break-up of Fijian society under the pressures of European private enterprise (55, 31). He created, in 1876, the Native Regulations Board, which drew up the fundamental law affecting the native people. It made provisions for regulating native affairs with the power to make laws for the good government and well-being of the indigenous population. Many of the provisions of that board have been retained in the current Fijian Affairs Ordinance with only slight modifications (52, 2). The Fijian Affairs Board superseded the Native Regulations Board.

For the purposes of the Fijian Administration, the Colony is divided into fourteen provinces based on old tribal territories. Each province includes a number of *tikina* which comprise groups of villages. In direct charge of each province is a *roko-tui*, usually a chief, appointed by the Government. He is virtually Provincial Governor of the Fijians. He is assisted by a Provincial Council which, meeting at least once a year, deals with all matters affecting the Fijians. Its formal resolutions, if approved by the Fijian Affairs Board, have the force of law. The Provincial Council decides the taxes, including school fees which are payable by all Fijians in the Province, and by those natives of the Province who are absent earning a living elsewhere.

At the head of each *tikina,* of which there are 76, is a *buli*—usually a chief whose rank or ability or both commands the cooperation and respect of the people. He is appointed by the Fijian Affairs Board. The *buli* is head of the District Council. He is assisted by a constable, paid by the Province, who, under the direction of the *buli,* collects statistics and taxes, and supervises village activities. The District Council has charge of making and repairing trails and bridges, house building, and planting food crops; it is also responsible for sanitation, especially as it relates to the cleanliness and health of the village (45, 231). Under the Fijian Affairs Ordinance, power is given to the *tikina* councils to make orders, and to provincial councils to make by-laws, concerning the welfare and good government of the Fijians within their respective spheres. Such orders or by-laws have the force of law when sanctioned by the Secretary for Fijian Affairs. At the bottom of the scale is the *turaga-ni-koro,* the village headman or chief, who with the advice of a village council directs all village communal activities.

Each Province has its own treasury, and the Provincial Council imposes its own taxes which vary from £3 to £6 per annum for every male adult. Fijian males maintaining five or more children pay a lower rate until the boys become taxpayers at eighteen. Other direct taxation is restricted to school rates, which, in some provinces, are collected separately from provincial rates (56, 568).

The Fijian Administration is, therefore, entirely an ethnic one and, even in provinces where the population is very mixed, it deals only with Fijians (16, 29). It is a state within a state, governing native life at all levels from the village to the province. In fact, therefore, there are two administrations in each of the fourteen provincial districts into which the colony is divided (16, 30). In some areas, populated mostly by Indians, the Fijian Administration is responsible for only a small fraction of the local population. Side by side with it, there is a District Administration which deals with the people of other races (4, 130). The District officers of the Central Colonial Government are discouraged from taking any direct part in the affairs of the Fijian Administration, except for a few minor things (16, 30).

The most influential organization in the administration of Fijian affairs is the Council of Chiefs. It also wields power and influence over the Central Government of the Colony, for it elects the five native members of the Legislative Council (16, 29). It submits to the Governor, recommendations and proposals for the well-being of the native people, especially those dealing with their government. All bills relating to important matters affecting Fijians are required by law to be referred for consideration to the Council of Chiefs and/or the Fijian Affairs Board before their introduction into the Legislative Council. The Council of Chiefs is the apex of the administration of native affairs, and the Fijian Affairs Board is its executive arm (16, 16ff.). There is a meeting of the Council of Chiefs at least every two years. It is the most important event in the Fijian world. The Governor of Fiji formally opens it, and the Secretary for Fijian affairs presides.

The Council of Chiefs was composed originally only of high chiefs who held important positions in the administration of native affairs or in other capacities. But its membership is no longer exclusively chiefs, for commoners who now hold important administrative or other positions in provinces are included. It consists of *rokos,* one or two representatives from each province elected by the Provincial Council according to the number of Fijians in that Province, a Fijian magistrate, a native school teacher, a Fijian medical practitioner, three representatives from urban-areas nominated by the Secretary for Fijian affairs, and six chiefs appointed by the Governor (56, 568). However, the Council of Chiefs overwhelmingly represents the attitude of the chiefs of the Fijian people, and has done so since its establishment in 1876.

The Council of Chiefs and the Central Government of

the Colony constitute a sort of interlocking directorate over the Fijian people. The colonial government is the prisoner of the chiefly aristocracy, just as in early Victorian times the Government of England was the prisoner of the aristocratic class (6, 10). It was taken prisoner in Fiji in the early days of the colonial administration and has remained so since then. It was apparent that the colonial government, if it was to rule at all, would have to do so with the consent of the Fijian chiefs. They got good positions under the British, who have always governed the native population by indirect rule.

Chiefs hold the majority of the principal posts in the Fijian administration. The Deputy Secretary for Fijian affairs and 11 of the 13 *roko* shown in the Fijian Administration Civil List for 1959 are of chiefly rank, as are all of the Officers of the Department of Economic Development and eight of the Fijian magistrates (16, 16). Furthermore, the five Fijian members of the Legislative Council of the central government of the Colony, who are regarded as "unofficial" members are in fact salaried officials of the Government (4, 129). They are all also members of the Fijian Affairs Board.

The Chiefs, then, through the Council of Chiefs, the Fijian Affairs Board, and the Legislative Council, have committed the native people to the traditional social and economic system. The Fijian administration in general, during the last decade or two, has become more and more entrenched as a completely exclusive and autonomous administration, divorced from the Central Government (16, 32).

The chiefs have great power as members of the Native Land Trust Board, an autonomous body independent of the control of the central government (16, 16, 22). It was set up in 1940 under the Native Land Trust Ordinance which was enacted "to set aside and proclaim as a native reserve" some of the land belonging to the Fijian people, and to demarcate and proclaim native reserve land. The work was estimated to take about two years (16, 23). Under the Native Land Trust Ordinance, lands not needed or likely to be needed by their Fijian owners are held in trust by the Government, and made available for leasing to applicants, whether Fijians, Indians, or people of other races (27, 21, 141).

The Native Land Trust Board has control over all Fijian lands leased or licensed outside reserves, and approves of all transfers of land and mortgages of leases. Its main functions are to approve or reject applications for leases, to assess rentals, and to collect and distribute rents (55, 17). It protects the interests of Fijian owners by reserving sufficient land for their use; it secures continuity in policy and security of tenure, and obtains for the native owners adequate rents for such of their lands as are leased. The Board pays the various *mataqali* the rents collected, less its own charges (16, 21, 22).

So far as Indian lessees who leased lands from native owners are concerned, many leases that expired have been taken into Native Reserves under the Native Land Trust Ordinance. No provision was included in the Ordinance for payment of compensation for improvements to the outgoing lessees, mostly Indians, who have found it difficult to secure other land to settle upon and cultivate (41, 10). When reserves have not yet been demarcated, the practice is to refuse renewals of leases of native lands as they fall due, and to allow tenants to remain at will on yearly agreements. Indians who operate such lands are, therefore, kept in suspense (16, 25).

Even if Fijians are not using their lands fully, the chiefs are very reluctant to see native tracts alienated. Their fear for their land is justified, for as already stated, Europeans in the early days got possession of much of the best land of the Colony, some of it under doubtful claims. In 1907, when an ordinance was enacted which permitted the sale or lease of communally owned Fijian land to individuals, shortsighted Fijians were willing to sell their land for immediate profit. All ordinances permitting such sales were repealed in 1909 (4, 139).

The Colonial Sugar Refining Company, a large and important Australian concern, has exercised considerable control in the affairs of Fiji, including the central government of the Colony. An old-time British resident in the islands remarked to me, "The government of Fiji has been run by the CSR and the big businessmen of Suva." The company has a capital of about twenty-one million Australian pounds (18, 7). It is the landlord for half the total acreage used for sugar cane, leases it to Indian sugar cane growers, is responsible for the transport of cane to its mills, for services to its lessees and other farmers, for manufacturing sugar, storing it, and seeing that it is transported to the market.

A commission of inquiry appointed by the Governor of Fiji in 1960, "to suggest the way back to peaceful conditions in the sugar industry," criticized "severely" the CSR for the way it handled the growers during the labor troubles of 1959 and 1960; the main blame was placed on the board of directors in Australia (18, 8, 9). It has contributed to the general industrial unrest in the colony by an attitude of paternalism, and the effect of remote control from its head office in Sydney. It is maintained that the company's senior European officials are lacking in a "sympathetic human approach to problems affecting the sugar industry," and that the public relations of the company are "archaic" (4, 178, 179).

The sugar inquiry commission recommended that the activities of the CSR should be handed over from the present Fiji division, based in Sydney, to a wholly owned subsidiary of the company with headquarters either in Suva or in Lautoka, the two larger towns of the Colony. It furthermore reported that the company would have an easier and more profitable time in Fiji, if it shared the responsibility of ownership of the industry with the local inhabitants (18, 12, 13).

Of the various factors affecting the administration of the Colony of Fiji, the dual system of government is the most disturbing, hindering its efficiency economically, socially, and politically. The Fijian administration exists side by side with a general administration and technical departments which cannot disclaim interest in matters which affect the indigenous people. There has been lack of cooperation between the Fijian Administration and the "productive" departments of the central government, notably the Department of Agriculture which has much to offer in the way of development. It has been authoritatively stated that the dual administration has stultified the economic progress of the Colony (16, 42).

For example, the Native Land Trust Board does not give the Department of Agriculture access to or control over some 40,000 acres near Ba, an area seriously eroded and deteriorated through misuse, unless it leases the land from the Board at an economic rent. The land is left to regenerate slowly under natural conditions, whereas it could be brought back to productive use much more quickly by controlled pasture and scientific management (16,

27). There have been no serious large-scale attempts by well-established techniques to develop fully the carrying capacity of the pasture land in the archipelago (41, 7). The cattle industry is not expanding as rapidly as it could (16, 44). The Colony is importing many commodities including essential food and dairy products which could profitably be produced locally (41, 11).

Growing bananas commercially by the Fijians also illustrates the difficulty of having two administrations in the Colony. It is an economic activity which necessitates close cooperation with the Department of Agriculture, but there is confusion between the Fijian Affairs Administration and that Department as to where the responsibility for various aspects of the project lie. Under the present system of raising bananas, the productivity of land used for that crop is bound to decrease (16, 44). It has been authoritatively stated that in the case of the Department of Agriculture, the department of most obvious importance to Fijian economic life, "frictions have been little short of disastrous" (55, 37). Overlapping of duties and friction over matters of jurisdiction occur in other departments of the two governments. Among anomalies of the joint administration is the fact that the districts of an agricultural officer, a medical officer, and other departmental officers do not in all cases coincide (16, 30).

PART V
Economic and Social

CHAPTER 7

General Economy

WITH the exception of sugar cane farming, many aspects of the economic development of the Colony, especially in agriculture, have been neglected. Yet agriculture is the basic industry, employing about 60 per cent of the total occupied population (16, 36). Exports in that field accounted for 85 per cent of the total export trade in 1958, a representative year. The proportions of the products shipped out were as follows: sugar and molasses, 63.75 per cent; copra and copra products, 19.93 per cent; bananas, 1.33 per cent; and hides and skins, 0.14 per cent (16, 36).

The sugar industry has grown in importance during the past decade. Indian cane-growers for the Colonial Sugar Refining Company increased from 8,687 in 1953 to 10,590 in 1957 (55, 18). Sugar cane is by far the most important crop in Fiji in regard to the amount raised, the yield per acre, and its value as an export, which is twice that of copra and bananas together. The whole economy of the Colony depends on this major industry which earns about £8 million a year, more than half of the total revenue. However, it can be little further developed in the foreseeable

139

future, for Fiji is restricted to a quota in the world's sugar market. The International Sugar Agreement puts a limit on the exports of sugar exporting countries of the world; and, therefore, on their production (19, 45). The acreage of sugar cane in Fiji has "more than reached" its uppermost limit and will not make any further appreciable increase in contribution to the general economy of the islands (16, 43).

The following figures for recent years illustrate the situation. The national basic allotment of sugar cane for Fiji for 1960, based on an export quota, and the amount to be sold locally was 1,532,300 tons. It was calculated for the production of 199,000 actual tons of sugar, the ratio of sugar cane to sugar averaging 7.7 to one (18, 41). The sugar export quota for 1961 was 170,000 tons (4, 191).

In 1962, 248,000 tons of sugar were manufactured, and 234,000 tons were exported. Sales of sugar in that year yielded about £10,000,000 as compared with some £6,300,000 in 1961 (15, 28). The estimate for 1963 was 2,145,000 tons of sugar cane to produce 275,000 tons of sugar. The harvest quota for 1964 was set at 2,300,000 tons of sugar cane and 300,000 tons of sugar (15). A British resident of Suva remarked to me, "When the sugar mills grind, there is plenty of money in circulation." The market is in New Zealand, Canada, and other countries of the British Commonwealth.

Due to the discoveries of the Colonial Sugar Refining Company which has its own research and experiment station, more sugar cane and that with a higher content of sugar is being grown on less land than before. At the time the sugar cane land at Nausori and the mill there were abandoned in 1959, at the end of that grinding season, the mill had been operating unprofitably for a number of years due to a) small crops much below its rated capacity, b) low content of sugar in the cane, for that district gets too much rain, especially at an unfavorable time for the growing crop, c) constantly rising costs of wages and materials, and d) a price of cane too high in relation to its sugar content (10, 3).

When I passed along Waila road in Nausori in 1960, thousands of acres of sugar cane had not been harvested. Some of the land had been cleared and was being used for rice farming; part of the old mill was used for hulling rice. Another abandoned area had a cacao plantation. A thousand Indians had to re-orient their means of livelihood by raising those or other crops. I visited the area with the Director of Agriculture who was helping them to make new uses of the abandoned cane land. In the Nausori district, 82 Fijian households and 745 Indian families were wholly dependent on sugar cane farming for a living; and 11 Fijian families and 257 Indian households were partially dependent on that crop (10, 3).

The Indians, most of whom are illiterate, don't understand the quota system, and seem to think they should grow as much sugar cane as they can, and that the company should buy it all from them. Sugar cane farming has earned them the largest amount of money for the least effort. It is also the crop most readily accepted as security for a loan (10, 3). Some of the Indians have used all their land for the production of cane and bought their vegetables in a local market. When they have contracts with the CSR, they know that their market is assured. Furthermore, many of them don't know how to raise another commercial crop, and if they did, they wouldn't know where they could sell it. In the summer of 1960, while I was in Suva, the farmers wanted the CSR to take eighty per cent of the sugar cane of each farmer. The company, however, maintained it could buy only seventy-four per cent of the May estimate of that year as recorded for each grower in the company's books (46).

At the end of 1960, the sugar inquiry commission ordered by the British Colonial Office in London, recommended setting up a Sugar Advisory Council to advise the company, the mill workers, and the farmers. It also recommended the establishment of a sugar board which would help arrange annual quotas. Its report stated that Fiji should be allowed to export to the United Kingdom 50,000 more tons of sugar a year than the quota then established. A very important recommendation already implied (see page 134) was that the sugar milling activities of Fiji should be handed over to a wholly owned subsidiary of the Colonial Sugar Refining Company in the Colony (18).

As for coconuts, bananas, rice, and various other crops in the Colony, there is room for further development. The preparation and export of copra was Fiji's earliest industry, beginning with the first European population; it still ranks high after sugar and gold mining. There is land owned by the Fijians available for coconuts, but much of the potential profits of copra from the land they use is "slipping through their fingers" because of careless methods of production (16, 56). The market for that product, although world prices fluctuate, is likely to last into the indefinite future. It has been authoritatively stated (16, 43) that 65 per cent of the coconut acreage of the Colony is in a state of declining productivity. The groves are untidy and uncared for; very few Fijians use cattle or goats in them to help in keeping down weeds and underbrush. As is the case with most small producers of copra in the Pacific islands in general, Fijians suffer from the lack of satisfactory copra-drying methods. Smoke driers in Fiji are very unsatisfactory and the production of clean, well-dried copra is not regarded as worthwhile. It is not graded, but is bought as "hot-air dried or fair merchantable" and very little first class material is produced (67, 9, 23).

There is plenty of land available for bananas which at one time occupied a high place among local products. The export of green fruit began soon after cession (27, 169). The chief hindrance to development is lack of proper and dependable shipping facilities, for the schedule of boats is uncertain, sufficient space on them is often unavailable, and there is poor ventilation for the perishable cargo. The New Zealand trade has been organized on a quota basis, and efforts are being made to open up trade with Canada. Nearly all the fruit now exported is produced by Fijians.

Rice is being grown in increasing quantities, and there is considerable land available for expansion. Low, flat areas of the Dreketi plains are well-suited to it. The basin of that river is intersected by numerous tributaries between strips of alluvial land. In many places the grade near the river is so slight that the waters are lost or dissipated in small lakes and swamps which could be drained without much difficulty and the land used for that irrigated crop. There is a big local market for the cereal.

Tobacco grows well in Fiji. Its commercial production is under the control and guidance of the Department of Agriculture. The product has a ready sale among Fijians and Indians; cigars are manufactured for local consumption, and the Fiji Tobacco Company has a factory in Suva. A pineapple industry has been re-started with prospects of canning.

Stock raising could be profitably combined with crop

production to the mutual advantage of both. There are at least 100,000 cattle and 20,000 pigs in the archipelago. Dairy cows are found in greatest numbers on Viti Levu; Vanua Levu has also a large count; there are hundreds on outlying islands. Working bullocks, widely distributed in sugar cane districts, are also used as draft animals in small-farming areas. The greater numbers of pigs are on the smaller islands, with Viti Levu second, and Vanua Levu third (Table 26).

Diversified agriculture could be developed much more than at present, for Fiji is well suited physically to a very wide range of crops. There is much needed diversification of Indian farming, which has hitherto been too much wedded to cane, with rice as a poor second (55, 18). In view of their increasing numbers, those colonists should look for land other than the best cane growing land which they now consider essential for farming (4, 113). Further encouragement should be given to develop dairying and associated industries, and to the cultivation of cotton, cocoa, coffee, pineapples, maize, and other cereals (41, 16). The Indian peasant finds it hard to initiate anything new in his procedures and operations, but the success of some of those who have attempted diversification should be an incentive, and the Department of Agriculture takes special pains to assist in that way. Much of the Rewa delta land, abandoned for sugar cane, could be used for beans, pulse, peanuts, coffee, and other crops.

The utilization and further exploitation of the extensive forests of Fiji have lagged behind developments of the Colony in other directions. Although timber is one of the principal natural resources, about half the requirements of the archipelago are imported. Forests are regarded as a wasting asset (16, 87). For most of the hill country of

Fiji, the best use of the land is for forests. Saw-milling could be expanded to mill the large quantities of logs which Fijian land owners of forested areas are capable of supplying. Unfortunately reckless clearing for gardens and plantations, and indiscriminate felling for house timber by Fijians have ruined much originally good forest country. There is a strong case for much more stringent control of conservation especially within the native reserves. (55, 73).

Progress in forestry is severely hindered by frequent fires which generally occur from July to October; they have raged incessantly for fifty years. It may be too late to rectify most of the damage done by them. "It would take more than the Colony's total annual budget to bring about a successful rehabilitation of even a portion of the area affected." It is necessary to adopt "a rigorous system of punishment by imprisonment" of those responsible to stop their occurrence. "Unless action is taken soon, the voices of those crying out against these recurrent fires will be like those crying in the wilderness—that one day large areas of Fiji will be" (10, 19).

There is a general abuse of land in the Colony which takes the form of improper cultivation, overstocking, and indiscriminate burning of brush. Many fertile parcels of Fijian lands leased to non-Fijians have been reduced to barren wastes over a short period of time by ruthless exploitation. There are large areas of sun-baked land on the main islands of the group (17, 6), and there is "appalling erosion" on market gardens near Suva (16, 62).

One of the more urgent problems of agriculture, not specifically Fijian, but of great importance to the people of the archipelago in general, is the "truly appalling state" to which burning, overstocking, and bad cultivation have reduced the soil in much of western Viti Levu. There has been sheet erosion of great intensity in parts of the hinterland of Nadi and Lautoka (55, 97). Some of the land is ruined beyond repair for the present generation of both Fijians and Indians. Extensive areas owned or leased by the Colonial Sugar Refining Company are much eroded through heavy and indiscriminate overstocking of cattle, while at the same time the CSR manages efficiently with a minimum of erosion a large beef ranch not far away from them (16, 53). A soil conservation program is urgent for all parts of the populated islands (55, 16).

In many areas, damage by recurrent floods is aggravated by soil erosion. Not only does this destroy the vegetative cover, which tends to absorb the rainfall, slowing down the runoff water from the hillsides, but it also silts up the river beds and forms bars across their mouths. They are thus less able to carry flood water to the sea; it backs up over agricultural land. At one time sailing vessels from Suva could anchor near the Ba bridge, but now trucks drive into the bed of the river at low tide to load sand and gravel (10, 15).

There is no fisheries' officer in Fiji, notwithstanding the fact that in 1946 the Secretary of State offered to support an application for a colonial development and welfare grant to provide for such a government offical (16, 85). Until very recently nothing has been done to develop the possibilities of local fisheries. However, it was decided in 1963 to allow a Japanese fishing fleet to be based at Levuka, and to set up a freezing plant and a fish meal factory. A license was granted to the Pacific Fishing Company, Ltd. to undertake the freezing and treatment of fish for export (15).

In addition to gold and manganese mentioned earlier (p. 68), other mineral resources of Fiji remain to be exploited. In 1958, the Fiji Geological Survey attained Departmental status, and five geologists were employed. Since then considerable progress has been made in regional geological mapping, the results of which are being recorded on printed maps and in descriptive bulletins (13, 1). In 1963, the Geological Survey Department of Fiji produced the first full report on the economic geology of the Colony (15).

The ownership of all minerals in the Colony is vested in the Crown, and so the Government is virtually a partner in all mining ventures. The first shipment of iron ore, from a deposit at Tuviriki, was made to Japan in 1958, and a trial shipment of hematite from a mine at Taci was made to the same destination. Production of copper ore from the Nukudamu mine commenced at that time, and shipment to Japan of 130 tons contained about nineteen per cent of the metal. The mining industry that year, including the yield of gold and manganese, contributed a total of £38,798 to Government revenue (14, 12). Miners continue to be in correspondence with overseas buyers in an endeavor to get prices for products of the mines sufficiently high to cover the cost of transportation. For most of the minerals which are found in Fiji, that is the main problem.

Manganese mine owners with marginal mines have only intermittent success in their operations, and some of them have gone out of production. One difficulty is that of obtaining a consistently high grade ore to meet the exacting specifications imposed by buyers of ore abroad. The larger mines, at Nasaucoko, Nabu, Vunamoli, and Koroviko continue to produce ore with a fairly high per cent of mineral content (14, 12).

The Emperor Gold Mining Company, Ltd., continues

to be by far the largest mining operator in the Colony. General and special developments are going on: sinking new shafts, stope making, and exploitation of new levels. The price of gold has remained static since 1939, but mining costs have increased considerably since then (14, 13). Government assistance has been sought and obtained to ensure the continued life of the Tavua gold field, where so many Fijians are employed (p. 68), and where they are specially looked after.

Fijians constitute more than half the total number of miners in the Colony. Indians are second and part-Europeans third (Table 12). The following table gives the number of people employed in the mining and quarrying industries according to ethnic group (14, 20):

TABLE 12

ETHNIC DISTRIBUTION OF MINERS

	1954	1955	1956	1957	1958
Fijians	1,351	1,367	1,851	1,629	1,494
Indians	289	340	656	523	447
Europeans	98	90	118	111	98
Part-Europeans	201	130	192	155	158
Others	133	164	188	173	201
TOTALS	2,072	2,091	3,005	2,591	2,398

Tourism in Fiji has expanded during the past decade to be the fourth industry in importance in the Colony, only surpassed by sugar, copra, and gold. It brings in a revenue of about a million pounds annually. Between 1958 and 1962, the number of visitors increased from about 12,000 to 18,000, and in 1963 it reached 24,000 (15). The big handicap is the shortage of hotel accommodation, which sometimes results in visitors being turned away. Rooms often have to be reserved months ahead. That situation is being remedied by the construction of new hotels, and the expansion of existing ones. The facilities of Nadi airport have been extended to equip it to accommodate jet airliners and their passengers. More and more visitors are arriving by sea. An increasing number of travel agencies in Australia, the United States, and Canada are including Fiji in what are known as Pacific "package tours." These include visits to Hawaii, Fiji, Tahiti, and New Caledonia (2).

The attractions of hot springs for visitors to Vanua Levu island have not yet been exploited. They are found in many localities on the Dreketi Plains throughout that part of the island from the Wainikoro River to Wainunu and Savusavu. Nearly all of them are less than three hundred feet in elevation; many occur in the beds of streams and on the shore between tides. Their waters vary considerably in temperature from warm to boiling point (27, 245).

The improvement of interior communications on Vanua Levu is necessary for the development of tourist attractions, and the same thing may be said of Viti Levu. More roads could be constructed to the interiors of these islands from the coast thoroughfares. The routes would also be of special benefit to Fijians and others for marketing their produce. An important factor hampering more direct Fijian participation in marketing is the poverty of communications (55, 49). Growers of *yaqona* and food crops in Magodoro *tikina* in Ba can get their produce out only by pack horses to the roadheads at Vakabuli behind Lautoka or Moce south of Ba (55, 49). The landings for flatbottom boats at farms along the lower Rewa are much in need of repair. In connection with ocean transportation, improvements of Suva wharf and its surroundings have long been neglected (16, 103). The wharf is important for unloading imports and for assembling exports.

The economy of Fiji as it relates to international trade is summed up in the imports of the Colony and their sources, and the exports and their destinations. The imports are similar to those coming into the Pacific islands in general. (See Tables 27 and 28, for detailed list.) Nearly all of them import flour, and bran sifted from flour (pollard). Meat is for Europeans and for natives who can afford to buy it. The indigenous populations are fond of canned fish, for the fresh product soon spoils in the hot climate. Imported pine and fir are more easily procured and more suitable for materials of construction than native hardwoods in forests difficult of access. Oil has not been found in any islands, so all the motor fuel comes from abroad, also all machinery and transport equipment. Fiji in common with many other islands in the Pacific lacks fertilizers. All fabrics come in from industrialized countries.

Nearly all the islands in the Pacific have one export in common, namely copra for coconut oil, and for many of them it is the only marketable product.

Fiji expresses the oil from some of its copra. Both Fiji and Hawaii send away raw sugar, and they also export fruit. The chemicals and other manufactured goods appearing in Fiji's detailed list of exports are re-exports of imported materials.

For many projects of improvement in the colony, capital expenditures are necessary (41, 20). Some land development schemes have had to be abandoned for lack of finance (17, 8). More rural credit facilities are needed (1, 334). It is authoritatively maintained that more of whatever

Fijian capital is available should be kept at home rather than invested abroad. "While Provinces are crying out for quite small sums to finance immediate developments, a third of some £600,000 of Fijian capital is invested in general Fijian Government loans, and two-thirds in developing the continent of Australia, while the merest fraction . . . is invested in specifically Fijian development. . . " (55, 66). Funds are specially needed for draining the considerable area of low, swampy land on Viti Levu. An indirect cause of poor drainage is short-term leases, for there is no continuing security for the lessee of land needing attention (16, 78). This is one of the drawbacks of agriculture in general. The period allowed Indians is generally too short, and, as a result, the lessee adopts wasteful methods, exploiting the land injuriously, and taking from it all that he can before the contract expires. Only leases for at least thirty years are satisfactory for Indians or Fijians (55, 99). A regulation which now prohibits leasing reserved land to people other than Fijians has resulted in some areas formerly leased to Indians and cultivated by them reverting to bush (16, 25). Apathy toward raising cacao trees is closely related to the unsatisfactory land tenure system in the Colony (16, 65).

It is difficult to make any categorical statements about the development of markets abroad, and consequent increase of exports. As already pointed out, there is an assured market for a certain quantity of sugar, for copra, gold, and perhaps some minerals. Markets for fruits, vegetables, and other products are uncertain, but more could be done to find new ones and to stabilize the situation. The following table giving the figures for the agricultural exports of Fiji in 1960 is representative:

TABLE 13

AGRICULTURAL EXPORTS OF FIJI, 1960

		QUANTITY
Bananas	cases	201,075
Melons	lbs.	249,017
Vegetables (Misc.)	lbs.	1,309,189
Fresh Fruits	lbs.	104,239
Copra	tons	2,499
Coconut Oil	tons	17,985
Coconut Cake	tons	8,398
Sugar (Unrefined)	tons	219,109
Molasses	tons	50,465
Peanuts	lbs.	69,855
Rice Bran	tons	177
	Miscellaneous	
Hides	nos.	10,307
Trocas Shell	tons	71

As for the home market, many commodities are imported which might be produced locally (16, 50). Some of them are suggested in the table of imports (Table 27).

A psychological factor in the economy of the Colony, difficult to measure, is the indifferent attitude of the indigenous population to the economic development of the archipelago, and their apparent inability to develop their lands themselves. Nevertheless, since agricultural work is their only hope of salvation in the indefinite future, sufficient land must be kept available for them. "With the Fijian outstripped in numbers and in commercial enterprises, the land in his possession is his sole hope of economic advancement, and to be without this in his own country would be disastrous" (17, 6). On the other hand his lack of capital equipment, the communal demands which weigh upon him, and, most important of all, careless cultivation, are his undoing. One of the Fijians said to me, "We know that it is better to weed the coconut plantations and the banana lands, but it's just too much work." This attitude, as already pointed out, is contrary to that of the Indians.

CHAPTER 8

Social Factors

AMONG the social factors affecting the welfare of the Colony of Fiji, various aspects of education are among the more controversial. Ethnic segregation in the schools, insufficient educational facilities for some thousands of children, and the relative proportion of the expense of schooling borne by the government, come up for frequent discussion among the people in general. Schools separated on such lines are a handicap to mutual understanding, and to the friendly relations that should exist between the different ethnic groups (16, 109). The chairman of a commission of inquiry into the economic and social situation in Fiji stated that "the existence of racial schools is unnecessary and harmful" (16, 4, 219). Schools are segregated largely on the basis of ethnic origin, religion, and language (41, 21); the government has three budgets for education—for Europeans, Fijians, and Indians.

The ethnic classification of schools in the Western Division of the Administration is representative (10, 28).

The Fijians do not want integration in the school system, for they foresee their children left behind in competition

TABLE 14

ETHNIC CLASSIFICATION OF SCHOOLS, WESTERN DIVISION

	GOVERNMENT	AIDE BY GOVERNMENT	RECOGNIZED	TOTAL
Fijian	2	65	6	73
Indian	6	78	7	91
European	—	4	2	6
Chinese	—	1	—	1
Mixed	—	5	1	6

with Indian and European students. But the need for improved educational standards among them is very evident. Many boys are so poorly grounded in elementary arithmetic that they cannot make good use of skilled and patient instruction at more advanced levels (55, 97). In contrast with the Indians, the Fijians are not interested in learning English. In 1959, for the first time, the address to the Council of Chiefs was read in English; since their Council was constituted in 1877, all the speeches and deliberations had been exclusively in the native vernacular (17, 3). The education of Fijians constitutes a problem because of their own attitudes. Many boys who leave school at fourteen, and are not taxable until they are eighteen, when they have to work to earn their tax, spend the intervening time in indolence and sometimes in mischief (53, 166).

The biggest problem of education is the lack of schools and teachers for thousands of children, mostly Indians. The simple statement of fact is that the Government cannot afford the expense involved in providing all the facilities necessary. Compared with other fields of government, the expenditure of the Colony for education in 1960 was £1,179,411; for medical and health services £844,881; for agriculture £238,124, and for forestry £85,794 (4, 125) The time has not yet come for free and compulsory education throughout the Colony (16, 109).

Of the total of 540 schools in Fiji, the government directly controls and is responsible for thirty-eight: ten for Europeans, fourteen for Fijians, ten for Indians, and four where the pupils are of mixed ethnic origin (41, 23). The great majority of the schools are supported in part by the government, a good many by the missions, and by the ethnic communities themselves.

O.H.K. Spate, scholarly geographer, commenting on the education curriculum, stated that at a higher level it is unfortunate that secondary education is patterned on the New Zealand system, "political and constitutional," with a west European slant, instead of giving some idea of the historical processes of social integration, and the effects of intermingling of local cultures (55, 97).

In spite of linguistic difficulties, the Indians have built up their schools in advance of those of the Fijians. Of the former, 100 take children up to the eighth grade (class 8), but only 53 of the native institutions take them that far. Indian boys have little interest in agricultural education, in part because of the difficulty of procuring land, but also because they prefer to look forward to white collar jobs in Suva and other towns. A considerable number are employed in large British stores. They work for less than a European, have a cheaper standard of living, and are gradually depriving British boys in general of positions as clerks, assistants in shops, and in other capacities. Young Europeans born in the Colony have greater and greater difficulty finding positions as the years go on. They look forward more and more to careers in Australia and New Zealand.

Financially the Fijians in rural communities find it difficult to fulfil commitments to maintain their primary schools, and to contribute toward the salaries of the staffs. The obligation is on them to provide furniture and other educational equipment, to build the teachers' houses, and to contribute 25 per cent of the registered-teacher salaries. This burden appears too great for many school committees to bear, especially if the income for a village or district is derived from a communal source. The problem is acute, for example, when the price of copra is low. The maintenance of school buildings, and the provision of furniture are generally neglected to enable the people to meet the salaries required.

The problem of the administration of education in Fiji is complicated by factors of geography, race, and language. Since the inhabited islands of the archipelago are spread over a very large area, many schools can be reached only by boat. In the hills of Viti Levu and Vanua Levu, and those of other islands, they are accessible only by overland journey on horseback or on foot. The dispatch and return of an administrative form between Suva and remote islands of the Lau group frequently takes several months. Similar communications between Suva and distant villages on Viti Levu occasionally take several weeks (45, 233).

The multi-cultural nature of the population creates the problem of the media of instruction. The standardized dialect of one Fijian District, Bau, is used in all Fijian schools, but the Rotumans, 500 miles to the north, have their own language, a variety of Polynesian. As for the Indians, Hindustani is regarded as the *lingua franca* of the Colony. But Urdu, Tamil, Telegu, and Gujerati are the languages of schools in communities where those tongues are spoken (See Table 19).

In matters of health, the Indians are appreciably better off than the indigenous population. Tuberculosis, for example, has a much higher rate among Fijians. The Indians feed their young children on milk, while native babies suffer from malnutrition, their parents preferring to kill cows for beef. Notwithstanding Indian dissatisfaction with the department of health and general welfare, the Colony is well served at present, and no increase in recurrent expenditures of medical and health services can be justified (16, 108). While a good many Indians are fully qualified physicians, trained in modern schools of medicine, the Fijians, as well as the natives of most of the Pacific Islands, depend on assistant medical practitioners, graduated from Suva Medical School.

Much of the social organization of India has not been transferred to Fiji. The caste system of that sub-continent, for example, is almost nonexistent in the colony. The Hindus who came to Fiji belonged to various castes: high, agricultural, and artisan. A considerable number were members of low and untouchable castes (39,3). The first weakening, and indeed the major breakdown of the caste system, came on the journey from India to the Colony. As far as we know, little or no attention was given to it by the officers, cooks, and stewards on the vessels on which the immigrants traveled. In general, the exclusiveness of that social attribute in India would be well-nigh impossible to observe on an immigrant ship, for there could be no rigid segregation. The Indians on board were thrown together indiscriminately; they ate the same food from the same dishes. When the dishes were washed, a Hindu ate from one earlier used by a Muslim—something unheard of in India. Purity of food and denial of contact, mainstays of the caste hierarchical system, were abnegated.

When the immigrants reached the sugar cane plantations, priest, barber, potter, and sweeper were assigned to the same work. There was no differentiation of status, and there was no economic dependence of one caste on another as in India. Furthermore none of the sanctions used in India to maintain rules of behavior could be enforced in Fiji. I was told that occasionally an Indian who is very angry with a fellow Hindu will, if the latter is of lower origin, refer to his caste disparagingly. However, in the new country, and in a very different social environment, since the great majority of the Hindus are very willing to forget their ancient heritage, caste is a negligible factor in their life in general.

As already pointed out (Table 18), there are great religious differences in the Colony. The Indians carry on an active pious life similar to that of those in the land of their origin. An administrative assistant, in an annual report, drew attention to the number of Indian religious ceremonies and folk festivals observed in the Colony (10, 13). They are symbols of continuing Indianization and the sectarian quality of Indian beliefs. *Ramlila,* a dramatic reenactment of Rama's life as one incarnation of Vishnu is celebrated annually; the anniversary of his birth is also recognized. Hindu leaders come from many parts of the archipelago to take part in the *Srimal Bhagwat Katha,* which is held early each year. It features the reading of the 6000-year-old *Bhagwat* script, sometimes by Fiji-born Hindus who have studied in India for the priesthood. *Mariamman* cults also take their places in the annual scheme of events; they are in general folk survivals of the worship of female goddesses. Firewalking accompanies two of the *Puja* ceremonial offerings to gods. They and others also are organized in part as a means of making money. *Holi* is celebrated during the full moon with pomp and gaiety.

Sunni Muslims also observe their own religious festivals. They are not sternly monotheistic, but rather mystics who absorb saints, and, on the level of folklore, drift toward animism. Those more devout perform their traditional acts of worship several times a day. *Jagriti,* and other Hindu newspapers in the Colony publish editorials on these festivals, exhorting the Indians to refrain from drinking liquor and gambling during them, but rather to spend their time in devotional prayers and worship. All the ceremonies and religious observances of the Indians are very much apart from those of the Christian Fijians.

Breakdown of the Fijian Social System

Integrated with the problems of the health of the native people, their education, and indeed with nearly all the social and economic problems of the colony, is that of the breakdown of native society and the communal way of life. Education, improved medical facilities, a new religion, and attempts at modern agriculture have undermined the old social system. Under economic pressure, and the impact of very different ethnic cultures the traditional way of life has gradually but steadily changed. As already stated, the effects of the transition are most severely felt in the villages, where communal work falls heavily on the older inhabitants, those who remain while the younger people drift away. The outward evidences are ill-kept trails, untidy gardens and plantations and, most of all, houses in disrepair and dilapidation.

It is interesting to note that the desire for a house of

modern materials is the greatest single incentive for a Fijian to work. There are several reasons for this. The building and upkeep of houses in the traditional manner are time consuming: choosing the trees in the forest, felling them with primitive implements, procuring grass for thatch, weaving coconut leaves for walls, and making cord for binding, of coir from the husks of coconuts. Fijians state that twenty years is a good life for a well-built and properly thatched structure, but that the type of dwelling made now, generally by people who are not skilled like the old craftsmen, has a life of only about five years. Modern wood and iron houses are not so comfortable as the traditional well-built houses; they are much hotter in the heat of the day, and cool off more rapidly in the evening. A district officer reports, "Housing amongst the Fijians remains at a low standard but is improving, largely owing to the efforts of the Fijian Development Fund Board to channel expenditure into beneficial projects, the chief of which are housing and water supplies. The absence of lining to houses with corrugated iron roofs is prevalent, which accentuates the heat in hot weather, and the cold in cold, and is conducive neither to health or *comfort*" (10, 52). More modern houses are seen in the copra provinces, on Vanua Levu and Taveuni, than in other parts of the islands, for the natives there have more money to buy materials. Prestige is an urgent motive for a wood and iron building, for it is to the Fijian evidence of "progress" —success at something new. As among rural Africans in Kenya, a tin roof is a sign of wealth (36). Furthermore, traditional housebuilding for young Fijians not only takes much time, but also interferes with their chances to get away and earn a little money somewhere, somehow. As stated earlier, only about one-third of the Fijian houses have iron roofs.

There is a steady flow of young Fijians to the towns because of the social attractions, and their desire to be free from communal obligations. Few of those who have attended school to fifteen years want to stay in the village (55, 70). In conversation with a late "teenager" one day, he stated, "The people in my village have *mekes* and *tra la la* dances, too. But in Nadi it's rock 'n' roll. That dance hasn't got to my village yet; but the kava ceremony is still important there, and big wedding feasts." I was struck, among other things, by the fluency and correctness of the boy's English, something exceptional among rural Fijians. As already mentioned, for thc Colony as a whole, about 26 per cent of the men who have titles in their *mataquali* lands have left thcir own provinces to engage in work elsewhere (10, 55).

Fijians away from their villages, living in Suva, Nausori, Levuka, and other towns, resent very much paying taxes, school fees, and other dues to their home provinces in lieu of communal work as required by the native Code. It seems essential that the Fijians in Suva should be given some definite and tangible return for the school fees and other taxes that they pay to their home provinces. Some part of the Commutation Rates paid in the Capital should be credited to a Suva Fund instead of to their provinces of origin. "They are domiciled in domestic fact in Suva, if not in legal theory according to Fijian Regulations " (55, 75).

Young Fijians with initiative who have gone abroad for a higher education are very dissatisfied with their lot in a village when they return. There is no opportunity for them to make use of their learning. More and more of them are forming a discontented group to side with the Indians in trying to bring about economic, social, and political changes in the Colony. Throughout the disturbances of 1959 and 1960, there was pronounced anti-European feeling on the part of both Fijians and Indians (4, 181). In Suva, a kind of lower middle class of educated people is forming, many of them in government employ, among whom there is a "definite sense of grievance," deeper than personal frustration (55, 75). The social and economic gaps between high civil service workers who are chiefs, and able, educated commoners, are circumstances about which the latter complain bitterly. Furthermore, a concentration of duties and responsibilities on the shoulders of the few chiefs who are capable leaders in the modern situation, deprives those of non-chiefly rank of the opportunity for advancement and leadership. One of the higher chiefs in the archipelago stated, "There is an insufficient number of men at present available who are either capable of, or who possess sufficient initiative, effectively to carry out the responsibilities of leadership."

In the course of the break up of the village organization, the chiefs have lost much of the confidence of the people, who traditionally have been conditioned by hierarchial authority, and who have willingly deferred to the judgment of the hereditary, high-ranking class in all matters that concern their daily lives. Fijian chiefs have become a sheltered aristocracy, unable to lead their people in the new direction which modern circumstances demand.

The Commissioners Annual Report for 1958 states that there are many influences at work which are contributing to a change of emphasis in the organization of the social system in the Colony, influences which are prevalent throughout Fiji. Some of them are the effects of education, radio, and newspapers; the closer relationship which Fiji now has with the outside world, in part through the increasing influx of tourists; and the growing dependence on a money economy. The report goes on to state that among the more important factors are "the decline in the influence of chiefs, and the development of greater independence of thought amongst the people" (10, 54).

A very important point about Fijian Regulations is that they are based on the assumption that all Fijian society is founded on the village, and that the traditional rules and customs of village life must be observed, with certain exceptions or partial exceptions which are carefully regulated by Commutation Rates and so on. But the facts of occupation and residence are increasingly difficult to reconcile with that theory, for a large proportion of the Fijians are not now firmly rooted in a particular *koro* or village. There are many second and even third generation natives whose link with the land is tenuous; they earn a living and make careers on the same footing as Indians and Europeans or as anyone else in the Colony. The Fijian Regulations still apply to them! (55, 76).

Indeed the disintegration of village life has reached such a degree that the normal attitude of the people to the Fijian Administration is perhaps best described as "resignation." The Regulations include, for example, obsolete and unenforced laws. *Kere kere* of money or property above the value of five shillings is an offense against Regulation No. 10, Section 20, but that law is entirely a dead letter (55, 36, 98). An important factor in village, demoralization is the "frequency of speculation" or "definite embezzlement" by officials. Fijians still exercise their social right to share property including funds contributed in common (55, 37). "Cooperation to the Fijian means not the sharing of responsibility and authority by members of a cooperative society over the management of their affairs, and the democratic principle of one man one vote to secure this end. To him it has always meant the concentration of power in one individual, and the pooling of resources of all members, whenever the need arose to help one individual or set of individuals requiring aid within that society" (Council Paper 20/1951, p. 6, quoted in 55, 57).

The effect of leases on Fijian society has been very disturbing. A really demoralizing factor is the extremely unequal distribution of the rents, both as between different *mataquali* and within any one of them (55, 17). The Fijian hails with satisfaction the discovery that it is unnecessary for him to work, for he can pay his taxes and, in many cases, enjoy luxuries, from income derived from the rent of his lands. A high standard of living among many Fijians is due to rents paid by Indians and to their engagement in various economic activities.

In the sugar growing areas of the Western Division, for example, Fijians receive considerable money as rents from their lands. Receiving a regular income without doing any work has reinforced in the minds of these people the idea that life is easy and work is not necessary. This has had a very demoralizing effect on them (10, 331).

An unearned income of £200 to £300 a year for a chief who is head of a *vanua* (i.e., a land division in a *tikina*), whose normal needs are supplied within the village, and whose house is built by *lala* or personal service due him, engenders a great disinclination to work. The chiefs, the natural leaders of native society, are often debauched by easy money, while the commoners receive a pittance scarcely worth saving. Only now and then does a *Turaga i-*

Taukei (head of a *vanua*) devote a substantial part of his rents to helping his people (55, 17, 18).

In spite of the money received by the Fijians from the Indians, there is considerable prejudice against them on the part of the indigenous population. The Fijians see an originally immigrant people who, when they arrived, were poorer than they were, but whose children are now better off. Indian land hunger and the Fijian determination to retain their land have helped to widen the gulf between them. The Indians in general are contemptuous of native attempts at individual farming or look on them with indifference. Like the average European whom they imitate, they regard themselves as superior to the Fijians. On the other hand the Fijians have greater concern for preserving the native culture than they have for the commercial and industrial advancement of the Colony. Fijian attempts to exploit the Indians cause in the latter a sense of frustration; they become annoyed and scornful of the "Christian" native (5, 23). Lack of contacts between the two ethnic groups until relatively recently is due to several circumstances. The initial settlement of the Indians was in the "lines" of plantations. Later on they leased unoccupied land separate and apart from the natives. The policy of early governors of the Colony kept Indians and Europeans also from settling in native villages (56, 180). Most important of all has been the official policy of the government which, from the beginning, has separated the two groups administratively.

Socially the Indians and Fijians keep entirely apart. In rural areas, the former live in groups or settlements rather than villages. Their homes are clusters of houses scattered over leased farms where there is little spatial evidence of unity or cohesiveness. Those from different parts of India speaking different languages are in general mixed together. Hindustani is gaining ground as the *lingua franca* for all, though the Muslims cling to Urdu. The Indians have profited a great deal materially by release from the tight cohesion of the Indian village, and especially by freedom from the caste system. They have lost, of course, part of their traditional culture for something as yet indefinable. One of the customs of their old village life is specially preserved—"informal, yet responsible, panchayats" (1, 333), councils of older men in their communities, who settle minor disputes rather than have them taken to the courts.

The Indians have adapted themselves to the new natural and social environment with a certain esprit de corps, a new discovery of social cohesion, useful spheres of service for women as teachers and nurses, modernized agriculture and animal husbandry, and a sense of public duty, all of which offer a challenge to an ambitious community (40, 26). They sense the security of their position; they have confidence, born of increasing numbers, and of agricultural, commercial, and industrial success. They realize that they are indispensable to Fiji's future. They have also assurance in their British citizenship, and of the growing national importance of India (5, 21).

Indian Disunity

However, the Indians in Fiji are not a unified community. Their population has never been homogenous. Broad cultural variations consist of different languages, rules of marriage, religious rites, diet, and names. The ideological exclusiveness of the Muslim faith compared with the inclusiveness of Hinduism keeps members of those religions apart in Fiji as it does in India. There is almost total absence of intermarriage between northern and southern Indians since they don't speak the same language. Indians seem to find unusual difficulty in social cooperation—at least in any enterprise which extends beyond a settlement or group. There is little neighborliness among the groups, and small desire for the good of the common weal. They are unable to cooperate on a basis of mutual trust, and show little sense of collective responsibility for affairs in the Colony (40, 15, 29). Northerners, southerners, and Muslims have sufficient cultural differences to give their members the feeling of belonging to separate groups (39, 144, 155).

The Punjabis, mostly Sikhs, and the Gujeratis, tend to stand aloof from the other Indians in the Colony. The Sikhs are specially enterprising. Gujerati businessmen help each other, and combine to fight non-Gujerati competitors; they are more shrewd than other commercial men in Fiji. Some of them engage in real estate transactions, and other profitable businesses in Suva and outlying towns (39, 46).

The manager of a sugar cane plantation remarked to me, "The Indians mulct each other on every opportunity." There is little cooperation among them—much like the fissiparous quality of social life in India. A cooperative movement in Fiji is predominantly Fijian. There are 51 purely Fijian societies against five purely Indian, and 22 other or mixed; some 80 embryo groups are almost all Fijian (55, 55). Shopkeepers who give credit to their compatriots take advantage of their less literate clients, and "fleece them unmercifully"(4, 114). It is alleged that Punjabis and Gujeratis are particularly responsible. Almost all cane farmers live on borrowed money on which they pay interest at the rate of ten per cent. They sell cane to the CSR on credit, and final payment is usually made five months after the mill is closed (46). Thousands of Indians, pursuing old patterns of life, are in serious debt to money-lenders. A loan of £10 for six months sometimes carries from £2 to £4 interest; that is forty to eighty per cent per annum (55, 63). Men in comparatively poor circumstances spend extravagantly at the marriage of their daughters to incur debts which cripple them financially for the rest of their lives (4, 114).

Indian cane farmers are split into unions which, in some matters, are irreconcilable; several are implacably anti-CSR. Ten of them are often in disagreement in affairs which affect their smooth operation and common well-being. During the strike of 1960, some of them were not in favor of accepting the terms to which others agreed. The Labasa Kisan Sangh union and the Fiji Kisan Sangh signed an agreement to cut cane near the end of the strike. The Maha Sangh, one of the more influential Indian associations would not sign the agreement. The Punjabis, in their exclusive group, promoted their own ideas of a settlement. A Gujerati was an intransigent leader of a minority which held out for special terms to the bitter end. Disagreements between the unions seriously hindered the settlement of that deadlock. There are forty registered unions in the Colony, of which nine have a membership of under fifty (19, 20). They include organizations for sugar cane growers, sugar mill workers, bus and taxi owners, workers in the dairy industry, labor at the wharves, teachers, commercial and municipal workers (10, 7).

Many unions have been formed with political ends in view. Farmers and others who join them are affected by patterns of allegiances and oppositions among leading public figures of the Fiji Indian community (39, 11). Industrial disputes are in part due to personal antagonisms, and a struggle for supremacy by competing leaders. Indian politicians themselves support this allegation (4, 179). A missionary in the Colony remarked to me, "There is always a ferment of political opinion among the Indians." The predominant characteristic of their political life is "rivalry, factionalism, and schism" (1, 333).

Pressure of Population

A social phenomenon in Fiji of great import in nearly all the Colony is the rapid increase in population. While the birth rate has remained at about 39.6 per 1,000, the crude death rate has been halved since the second world war. It stands at 6.9 per thousand compared 11.7 per thousand in India. The success of the medical services in reducing the death rate, but not the birth rate, has been "an important contributary to Fiji's present economic difficulties" (16, 108). There was an annual increment in population of 2.91 per cent in each of the ten years between October 1946 and September 1956 (20, 5). Between 1946 and 1963, the population of Fiji gained an increase of 65 per cent (15, 118).

The birth rate per thousand Indians between 1954 and 1958 (Table 29) was about 44, that of the Fijians for the same period and number, 36. The proportion for Europeans in the Colony was 18, and for Euronesians, that is mixed unions between Europeans and Fijians, 32. The death rate for Indians was 7 per thousand, for Fijians approximately 9. The European ratio was a little over 4 deaths per thousand, and the Euronesian nearly 5 (Table 30).

In 1962 the population of the Colony increased by nearly 14,000; it was estimated at 427,851, compared with 413,

872 at the end of December, 1961. Fijians numbered 177,-770 compared with 172,455[1] in 1961, Indians 212,829 as against 205,068, and Europeans 10,553 as against 10,417. The estimated population of Fiji grew by 13,000 between June, 1962, and June, 1963. It was 421,000 in mid-1962, 427,000 at the end of that year, and 434,000 by the end of June, 1963 (15). The percentage of total population increase has grown since the early years of this century. In 1911 the average annual increase since 1901 was 1.5 per cent, in 1956 it was 2.91 per cent, and in 1962, 4.17 per cent (Table 31).

The proportion of the two main components of the population has changed significantly during the last two decades, and, as already pointed out the Indians now outnumber the Fijians. As early as 1907 their increase was officially noted. It was stated that in that year the natural increase of the Indian population was considerable; there were 1,195 births among the immigrants and 640 deaths. The birth rate was high, 38.6 per thousand, and the death rate was low; for indentured adults the mortality was 14.33 per thousand, and for free people 11.23 per thousand. The death rate for children of free immigrants was 44.32 per thousand; that for children on the plantations was 139.35 per thousand, the large proportion being of infants under one year of age (8, 87).

The Fijian population was markedly declining toward the end of the 19th century, and at the beginning of the 20th, as indicated in the following table; and from about 1907 on, there has been a steady increase.

---

[1] Another estimate is 171,248. The author found that estimates for certain years vary, perhaps according to whether the figure was taken for June or December.

TABLE 15
DECREASE IN FIJIAN POPULATION, 1881–1907

	YEAR	POPULATION
Census	1881	111,924
	1891	105,800
	1901	94,397
Estimated	1907	87,029
,,	1908	87,114

The diminution was principally due to "neglect of children, to the ignorance of the elementary laws of sanitation, and to the entire absence of all precautions against the spread of infectious or contagious diseases" (8, 85).

While the Indian birth rate is proportionally high, the Fijian rate cannot be considered low. In 1962 it was 37.27 per thousand as compared with 36.89 per thousand in 1961 (15, 35). A Fijian girl of sixteen was showing me about her home village one day when I asked her how many brothers and sisters she had. "Seven brothers and eight sisters," she replied. "I am the sixteenth, the youngest." "Your father had a large family," I said. "Yes," she answered sweetly, "but there were six mothers."

The increase in population coupled with retarded economic development has brought about signs of unemployment. Some people in need of means to earn a living are already found in urban and also in rural areas (41, 9). Indians out of work are vigorous agitators; aware that they are without prospects of betterment, "not unnaturally they become radical and revolutionary" (40, 30). In December, 1962, 118 people were registered as unemployed—the largest number in Suva, where 80 were looking for jobs. A total of 296 people registered as unemployed in Fiji in February, 1963. Work was found for 28 of them. Those who registered included 76 young people from schools, looking for their first opportunities (15).

Economic pressure is beginning to be felt in some families of chiefs. Their sons look for work, and daughters hire themselves out as maids in European families. The latter are more apt at being domestic in a modern way than commoners, are more intelligent, and more efficient helpers. Furthermore, they display the innate courtesy and dignity of their parents, traits which the author has observed many times.

PART VI
Prospect

CHAPTER 9

The Future

THE SOCIAL, economic, and political situation in Fiji is unstable, and over the next three or four years the problems will be grave and urgent. Severe disorganization of the Fijian socio-cultural system is being caused by the impact of a variety of forces, which are pushing the system beyond the limits of equilibrium. The strongest force is the conflict with the Indian ethnic group, which is resulting in extreme disadvantage for the indigenous people.

It is not possible to predict the conditions under which particular innovations in Fijian culture in general will occur, that is to say which of several possible modifications or changes will be made, and under what circumstances, for they involve considerations of personal motivation, idiosyncratic experience, cultural and situational milieu, and general cognitive processes. "In itself innovation is an 'instinctive' propensity of the human organism, activated under the merest provocation of desire for richer or more orderly experience" (61, 127). The motivation will consist of broad values, ethnic character, "model personality structure, such as the desirability of material wealth, the relative importance of kinship and community obligations, and the significance of punctuality" (61, 129). The dynamic role of loyalty to Britain will also in part determine the course of culture change. A Fijian member of the Legislative Council of the Colony, who is also a member of the Fijian Affairs Board, stated at a meeting of the Council in October, 1963, that the Board expressed the will of the Fijian people, "that their ties with Britain be made stronger" (15).

The fear of many observers is that if new institutions are not created and developed in the near future, a great struggle, even involving force, may arise and flame (1, 334). There must be constitutional changes to give the various ethnic groups of the Colony an effective voice in its administration. A substantial body of responsible public opinion among them advocates an orderly constitutional advance.

All authorities on Fiji agree that the whole philosophy of native life, as enshrined and enforced in the Fijian administration by its regulations, is inimical to the best interests of that ethnic group, and that, if the separate administration is not abolished, it will continue to handicap the native people severely in competition with the Indians and other people in the islands (15; 16; 4). Furthermore, the Native Affairs Department is an unnecessary expense which the Colony cannot afford; it is wasteful of manpower and money (16, 31). It should, of course, be given up gradually, but steadily. An Indian Secretariat parallel to the Fijian Affairs Board was abolished some years ago, at a time when it was hoped that the administration of the Colony would be centralized, but that hope was not fulfilled (41, 35). Although each of a number of districts has an Indian Advisory Council, it is for the most part, a figurehead. As long ago as 1913, it was authoritatively stated that the existence of the Department of Native Affairs was "no longer necessary or desirable" (4, 133). The Government and the Legislature have for too long adopted a paternalistic attitude toward the native population. They have given a too high priority to fostering the Fijian communal system, and the customs and observances traditionally associated with it (16, 38). Even as far back as 1908, Basil Thompson published a book on the Fijians, "bearing upon the state of transition from customary law to modern competition;" it was based on anthropological information collected in 1903 (57, v). Had the government, including the chiefs, got together then to gradually lead the people into the modern world, the situation today would be very different.

The sin against the Fijians is that they have always been pampered; they have never been up against any problems. They have been so bound by customary obligations, enforced by the Fijian administration and the chiefs that they have not had any opportunity to develop initiative. One of the higher chiefs in the archipelago, an old friend, said to me, "I am in favor of doing away with the Department of Fijian Affairs gradually. But some of the chiefs don't want to give it up. And many of the Fijian people want it too, for they are afraid they will be lost if there is no one to look after them."

The salvation of the Fijians must come eventually from the Fijians themselves, and most of all by a recognition of the supreme importance of work—regular, responsible, and efficient work, so as to enable them to compete successfully with others (51, 82). Their only path for survival is that toward individualism in agriculture. The objective must be a community of independent farmers, living and working on holdings heritable and alienable at least between Fijians. Shifting cultivation is unsuited to cash cropping, which requires continuity and intensity of effort on the same ground (55, 9). The preamble of Sir Arthur Gordon's Land Ordinance (XXI of 1880) looked forward to the time when the Fijians would be ripe for individual land holding, but this was lost sight of later in the century, the heyday of indirect rule and communal taxation in kind (55, 86). Sooner or later the problem of permanent titles to their land will have to be faced by the Fijians. The *galala* or peasant farmer is their only hope of salvation.

The first obstacle to independence of the Fijian is the communal ownership of land. But if he has overcome that, and secured an individual title to land by lease or agricultural license, he has the second handicap to face. If he is by blood a member of the community where he works his land, he has to conquer a more serious one, the latent hostility of the neighbors, and the demands they make in the traditional manner, to share his prosperity without contributing to it; he also sacrifices the good will of the chiefs. The leveling influence of public opinion is almost impossible for him to resist, and has a persistently retarding effect upon the progress of exempted men settled in their own provinces. They can avoid it by establishing themselves as individualists in another Province, but in doing so they have difficulty in securing an individual title to land there. The necessary solution, "if the Fijians are to play their proper part as agriculturists in the future economy of the Colony is to shift the emphasis, mentally, from the community to the individual as the most efficient productive unit. In the initial stage it is a psychological problem which requires a psychological approach" (10, 55).

In regard to bananas, for example, a government official reported that if a communal system in the production of that crop is to be successful, "compulsion is an essential ingredient to its success." Previously compulsion was in the form of orders from a chief. Now that the effectiveness of that form is declining, it must rest on the "compulsion of regulation, rigidly administered. . . This necessity for compulsion will continue until replaced by individual incentives, when the whole Fijian economy will change from being directed centrally from above, to a state where each individual, on his own initiative, accepts the advantage of working for his own benefit" (10, 56).

The Council of Chiefs as well as the Colonial Government will have to take considerable responsibility for what happens in the future. That Council recently went on record as stating, "The notion that the individual should be the basis of ownership is . . . premature, and is, therefore, not in the best interests of the Fijian people generally. It is recommended that the present system of Fijian land tenure, ownership, administration and reservation be rigidly maintained (17, 5). If the idea expressed in this resolution was not premature in 1903, how can it be regarded as premature in 1963! As already indicated, the Council of Chiefs carries great weight with the Fijian population. Its membership has always included representatives from all the Provinces, and it is regarded as the mouthpiece of Fijian public opinion (52, 3).

The chiefs will have to reorient the direction of their leadership. Through the Native Land Trust Board they have deliberately stalled until recently in not demarcating reserve land (16, 25). As already stated, the work was begun in 1940, and only now shows signs of being finished (15).

The Chiefs have given too much emphasis to the Deed of Cession of the archipelago in 1874 to Great Britain (26). Queen Victoria's representative at that time was Sir Hercules Robinson, later Lord Rosmead, then Governor of New South Wales. He explained to the chiefs that while the cession must be full and complete, they would be giving the islands "in a chiefly manner." They must "trust to the Queen's justice and generosity as their sovereign and highest chief to return to them all or whatever part of their gift she might think right." They must have confidence that she would govern them "righteously and in accordance with native usages and customs" (52, 1). The interpretation of the Deed by objective observers now is that it holds only until the people of the islands have learned to govern themselves.

The attitude of the Chiefs to the Report of the Burns' Commission is considered grave, in view of the fact that it is the result of the most thorough investigation of the economic, social, and political situation ever made in Fiji (16). The Commission worked in a thorough, conscientious, and realistic way, trying to fit today's inescapable economic and social facts to political conditions based upon sentiment and tradition. It made 124 recommendations, some of which are of far-reaching importance, and basic to the economic and social development of the Colony. The Commission strongly urged that all its recommendations should be put into practice together by the people of Fiji, for they formed a unified whole, and that it would be no good to take just those which appeal and leave others (16, 125).

The Burns Report, submitted as a "complete scheme" was emasculated by the Council of Chiefs by their non-acceptance of the principal recommendations (50, 57).

That Council informed the Governor that it would not accept the recommendation for the abolishment of the Fijian administration, and the merging of its powers in the Central Administration; it refused to accept the principle of taxation of Fijian lands which are not being effectively used, and also of taxing other revenues from lands (17). It accepted in principle, but only by a small majority, the direct election of three Fijian representatives to the Legislative Council (plus the two selected by their Council). Fijian chiefs have been reluctant to allow the commoners the same political privilege that is enjoyed by other ethnic groups in the Colony, namely the direct election of their representatives to the Legislative Council (4, 228).

Economic

The social and political progress of the Fijians must rest on a strong economic basis. There has never been a coordinated and continuous policy or program for the general agrarian development of the Colony, although "such a policy is long overdue" (16, 48). Future farming requirements will have to be anticipated.

The copra business could be greatly developed and bring much good to the Fijians. The industry is now important, but its future improvement requires careful planning as part of the whole economy of the Colony. Much good land for palms is still unused, and arrangements for the sale of coconuts and their products are haphazard. The consumption of coconut oil in the world is likely to increase, for it will hold its place among competing edible fats which are being more and more used as the population of the world grows. Copra in Fiji is about one per cent of the present world production. Groves of thirty acres should be made available for each Fijian grower, and he should have a 99-year lease (67, 24, ff).

For the Indians, security of tenure is an important problem to be solved. There is a great deal of misuse of land by them because of their insecurity in farming. The Indian does not improve the land and generally exploits it mercilessly (16, 25).

The Fijians must allow others to use land belonging to them which is not now being used economically, or which is not likely to be so used in the near future. The Director of Lands stated in the Legislature in 1940, "If I may presume to offer advice to the Fijians, I would say: Your duty to the state is not performed by keeping valuable land unalienated if it is not genuinely required for your use, maintenance, and support, nor is it performed by cultivating small, scattered patches in food crops in such a way as to keep out of commercial production considerable areas of land. Your obvious duty to yourselves and the community is to utilize to the fullest extent that land which can reasonably be reserved to you, and you should make available to others all land which is not genuinely required for your own use, maintenance and support" (41, 13).

Speaking in the Legislative Council when the Native Land Trust Bill was debated, the greatest native Fijian statesman, the late Sir Lala Sukuna stated, "Land owners have duties as well as rights. Travel the country and you see small patches of native cultivators here, long stretches of unused land there, further on, more scratchings. Is the native, is anyone, justified in holding up large tracts of land in an agricultural country with a quickly growing population?" (41, 12).

There is considerable non-Fijian land in the archipelago not adequately used. The Governor of the Colony stated before the Legislative Council in 1948 that he observed "thousands of acres of land lying virtually idle," and that some of it was land not occupied by the natives (41, 7). The Burns Commission emphasized the protection of "freehold" to any owner. It merely recommended that "all owners of land, whether freehold or communally owned, should be taxed heavily in respect of any land which is capable of being used, and which is not adequately used" (16, 27). However, the inviolability of freehold has not been an unalterable precedent set by the British Government at home.

Various land tenure experiments have been conducted in Ireland, some of which can be applied to Fiji, taking into consideration the different natural and social environments of the latter. The most important of the land purchase acts in Ireland, the Wyndham Act of 1903, induced the landlords to sell out. The sales were financed by advances made from an Irish Land Purchase Fund, raised on the market in return for government guaranteed 2 3/4% stock (49, 306).

When the Wyndham Land Bill was being argued in the House of Commons, the sponsor of the Bill stated, "All interests—landlord and tenant, Nationalist and Unionist, British and Irish, can hope for no tolerable issue to any view, constitutional, political, or economic, which they severally may cherish until, by settling the Irish land question, we achieve social reconciliation in Ireland" (49, 296). The same statement can be made in regard to the Colony, substituting the words "Fijian for "Irish" and "Fiji" for "Ireland." In Ireland the landlords had not realized the truth of the dictum: "Property has its duties as well as its rights" (49, 27).

Social

Social adjustments will follow new economic policies. The rule of village administration that natives have to devote part of their time to communal work will have to be changed. It has been authoritatively stated that "part-timing is one of the curses of Fijian life, and there is only one answer to it, that is more specialization within the village, and cash payments for work done on behalf of the common welfare." Village councils are at present "moribund" and only a complete change of policy will reinvigorate them (55, 2ff).

The phenomenal growth of population especially that of the Indians aggravates the economic and social problems of the Colony. The Indians have a strong lead in rate of growth, and even if their birth rate decreases within the next few years, the fact remains that, "of all the component populations, the Indian population has, inherent in its age structure, the greatest potential for increase" (55, 2). By 1971, it is estimated that the Indians will be more than 53 per cent of the total population.

The Fijian and Indian population in the future is officially estimated as follows (16, 10):

TABLE 16
FUTURE FIJIAN AND INDIAN POPULATION

YEAR	FIJIAN	PER CENT OF TOTAL	INDIAN	PER CENT OF TOTAL
1966	197,757	40.43	254,706	52.07
1971	227,663	38.99	314,366	53.84

A former census commissioner has estimated that, based upon the present rate of natural increase, the total population of the Colony will reach 500,000 by 1968 at the latest, and that by the year 2,000 the population will be between

GROWTH OF FIJIAN AND INDIAN POPULATION, 1881 - 1961

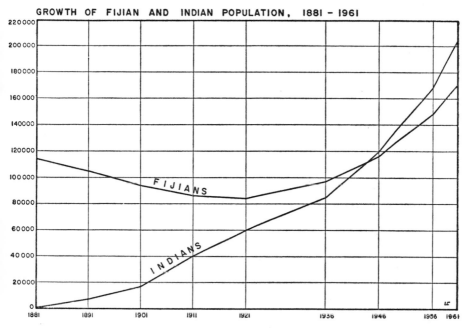

22. GROWTH OF FIJIAN AND INDIAN POPULATION (1881–1961). The Indian population's rate of growth is causing much concern to the native Fijians. While the native populace now numbers about 43 per cent of the total figure, the Indians represent approximately 50 per cent. The first Indians arrived from the subcontinent in 1879, as indentured workers for a period of five years.

1,200,000 and 1,400,000 (16, 7). For the near future with which the problems of today are most concerned, it is estimated that the total population may increase to 584,000 by 1971. The great growth to more than half a million souls must be seen against a background of very serious erosion and soil exhaustion, particularly in the more populous western plains of Viti Levu. Land will have to be used more intensively as population increases, and individual farming will lead to more continuous and intensive use of Fijian land. Whether or not the area of land in the Colony available for cultivation remains static, or perhaps, because of erosion, may be reduced, the population of the archipelago will keep on growing.

About 10,000 children in the Colony finish their schooling every year. Not more than ten per cent of them can find "white collar" jobs in the towns, so the remainder must expect to be employed on the land (15). Within the next five years, probably some 1,500 of the older Indian men will cease to grow sugar cane. That number constitutes only 12.5 per cent of the forthcoming population in need of employment.

The inescapable economic and social facts of Fiji are the insufficiency of available land, and of established industries to support the growing number of people. Lack of improvements in agricultural production, coupled with the difficulties encountered in extending the area of cultivatable land, could soon bring about a major unemployment problem with a further drift to the towns. There are many Fijians without land. They are bound to degenerate into the poorest class in the Colony if they cannot find employment (17, 6). In view of the increase in population, it is essential to develop new land. New farms will have to be established.

Bright Spots on the Horizon

The future of Fiji is not all dark for bright prospects have appeared on the horizon. In June 1963 a Government Order established six Local Development Boards which will play an important part in the urgent problem of developing Fiji's land. The Boards are charged with the task of drawing up development plans, submitting recommendations to the Government for land development and settlement, and with receiving applications for loans. Some District Officers will be employed full time on land development plans, while others will be progressively relieved as far as possible of other duties to enable them to give priority to that aspect of the future of the Colony. A capital expenditure of £20,000 was approved, and machinery pools have been set up from which equipment will be rented to farmers (15, 128). In short, Fiji's first large-scale land settlement scheme is getting under way. To assist its work, a soil survey of the islands has just been completed.

The Colony has planned to spend £3 million on capital developments. Some of the money will be provided by Britain in Colonial Development and Welfare grants; the rest will come from general revenue and loans. Loans have already been made to independent Fijian farmers engaged in diversified agriculture. Fiji's sugar cane farmers will be eligible for funds to make capital improvements on their farms (15, 5). In 1963 the Government announced schemes of subsidizing coconut plantations and native groves (67, 33).

A subsidiary of the Colonial Sugar Refining Company has been set up in Fiji, as recommended by the Commission of Enquiry into the sugar industry. That company, reconstituted into "South Pacific Sugar Mills, Ltd." has taken over the assets and activities of the CSR in the Colony. Among other things, the change makes possible a local examination of its books. The new subsidiary announced that the capacity of its sugar mills would be increased by some 11,000 tons for the 1964 season. It plans to spend a large sum on replacement and expansion, on buildings, and other equipment. It will grant tenancies to Indian farmers for terms of twenty-one years instead of ten years as heretofore. In line with its new spirit, South Pacific Sugar Mills, Ltd., has awarded twenty-three scholarships to children of non-staff employees to enable students to attend secondary schools of their choice (15, 38, 45).

An endeavor is being made by the Indian leaders in the Colony and people generally to encourage among themselves methods of birth control and family planning. Indifference is giving way to concern about the serious problem of overpopulation. It is considered the moral duty of those who contribute most to the increase to display a sense of responsibility in controlling their birth rate. A family planning campaign to slow down the rate of population increase is meeting with success (15, 199). The Medical Department is providing additional family planning clinics to advise and help those parents desirous of restricting the number of children in their families. Family planing advice has recently been made available at 55 centers scattered throughout the Colony (15). A large number of Indians are urging the necessity of birth control (16, 8). That way of slowing down the increase in population is now held as vital to the welfare of the Colony.

A significant recent political development in Fiji occurred in 1963—an amendment to the Constitution made possible by an Order in Council in London (15). The amendment provides, among other things, for the office of Governor, the setting up of a new Executive Council, and a Legislative Council, the office of Speaker, the making of legislation, and method of procedure in the Legislative Council. Under the Order in Council which was made at the Court of St. James in London, the Executive Council now consists of three ex-officio members; the Colonial Secretary, the Attorney-General, the Financial Secretary, and members appointed by the Governor. The three specifically mentioned are also ex-officio members of the Legislative Council.

The change in the Constitution provides for a Legislative Council of not more than nineteen official members, and eighteen unofficial members instead of fifteen as formerly; six Fijians, six Indians, and six Europeans. Of the unofficial members, four Europeans, four Fijians, and four Indians are elected on separate "racial" roles, two Europeans and two Indians are nominated by the Governor, and two Fijians are the choice of the Council of Chiefs, voting by secret ballot. The term of the Legislative Council shall be five years unless it has been dissolved sooner.

The electoral role was greatly enlarged. The franchise was extended to make nearly 100,000 people eligible to vote instead of about 16,000 as before. It was constituted that the Fijian people would directly elect four of their members, as compared with the past when, as already stated, the Fijian members were selected by the Council of Chiefs. For the first time the women of Fiji have been granted the privilege of voting.

An election under the new amendment took place in April 1963. Some 94,000 people registered as electors: 53,000 Fijians, 36,500 Indians and 4,500 Europeans. Polling began on April 17, and went on for ten days over the widely scattered islands of the group. A little over 81 per cent of the registered electors cast their votes: seventy-five per cent of the Fijian electorate, about eighty-seven per cent of the Indian, and eighty-four per cent of the Europeans (15, 80).

Great Britain's Under Secretary of State for the Colonies, visiting Fiji in 1963, reported he had "found quite considerable interest in suggestions that we [i.e., Fiji] should move towards internal self-government" (15). It has been proposed to hold a conference in London to draw up in that direction a new Constitution for the Colony. The British Secretary of State for the Colonies will consult with representatives of the people of Fiji in working out such a constitutional framework (15).

It has been proposed that local governments be instituted by elected representatives of the three major groups in the Colony: Fijian, Indian, and European (16, 30). These would train people in the methods of representative government. Set up area by area throughout the Colony, they would gradually replace the Fijian Administration. The majority of Europeans favor such a revision of the Constitution, but are reluctant to press Indian claims relating to administration and land ownership at the expense of the Fijians. They maintain that in rural areas, the well-being of the Fijians in the immediate future could best be left in charge of the District Offices (4, 133). The new conception of democratic government in Fiji insists on merging the present Fijian Native Administration with the Central Administration, and the gradual replacement of chiefly rule by the Fijian commoner's ballot-box.

The most hopeful outlook for the future takes in several instances the form of inter-racial cooperation on behalf of the welfare of the Colony as a whole. There is just the beginning of a sentiment and outlook which will gradually join the various ethnic groups and communities into a national unity. It is such a state of mind of cooperation which has largely contributed to the welfare of Hawaii, where the author spent 13 years in the Department of Geography in the University. It is the only long-time solution to the ethnic problems of Fiji. A Fijian member of the new Legislative Council stated in a recent speech "what we have got to look for in Fiji is unity—the unity of

the races" (15). A "multi-racial" club has just been formed
at Nausori near Suva to put into practice, "tolerance,
understanding, and harmony between the various races
in the Colony" (15).

In towns and along parts of the coasts there has been
considerable mixing of Fijians and Indians. In the former,
men of both ethnic groups fill the middle and lower posts
in government and commercial offices. There also, Indians
mingle with Europeans as fellow government servants or as
members of a single firm. They also meet each other in the
professions of medicine and law (39, 12).

Although there is less contact between rural groups,
some country districts provide good examples of inter-
racial cooperation when the making of a road or some other
project mutually beneficial is carried out. A Division Commissioner reports that in his area Indians and Chinese
pursue their own business in a quiet and effective manner,
"maintaining good relations with the Fijians amongst
whom they live," and that the Chinese have "become integrated with Fijians by inter-marriage" (10, 57). The
Fijians and Indians take advantage of the skills and
strengths of each other to achieve some common ends. They
have adopted various habits from each other, as for example the general drinking of *yaqona* by the Indians, and
eating curry by the Fijians (53, 163). Many Indians speak
a little Fijian.

Both races in nearly all parts of the archipelago have
encounters in the store, bus, hotel, cinema, market, and
in the town. In schemes of urban development, each has
paid attention to the ideas of the other. English is now the
common language of both, although as yet it is confined
to the educated minority (39, 180). Fijians working farms
adjacent to those of Indians who are raising similar crops

are observing the latter's methods of operation. The Fijian is learning the handling of livestock and much of his agricultural practice from the Indian.

Fijians and Indians work together in the Civil Service, Police Force, and in other walks of life with apparently little friction (16, 10). Fiji has a well-trained Civil Service, the result of education and training of Europeans, Fijians, and Indians over many years. It will continue to run efficiently during future changes in the government. In the "Water Rates" office, for example, which I visited one afternoon, there are four Europeans, four Hindus, two Muslims, and one Sikh. The chief of that office is a part-European whose mother is a Polynesian from Wallis Island. In 1962, the Police Force consisted of 422 Fijians, 227 Indians, 31 Europeans, 12 Rotumans, and 4 part-Europeans (15). A Fijian policeman who worked his way through the ranks was recently promoted to assistant superintendent of police for the Colony (15). These examples imply for the future a careful and purposeful administration to remove gradually and ultimately the cultural differences and prejudices which still exist. From many points of view the Fijian and Indian face the same problems, struggling to achieve a higher standard of living.

A little integration is going on in some schools, mostly secondary schools. A few children from other groups are being included in hitherto segregated educational institutions; it is being done quietly without any show of publicity. I visited the Suva Point "Boys and Girls Grammar School" where there are students of Fijian ancestry, European background and some of Indian blood. Gradual and regular integration of the schools will be an important factor in the future welfare of the Colony. A school system must be instituted which will indoctrinate children of all the ethnic groups with a loyalty to Fiji, and which will inculcate an acceptance of all of them as contributors to a modern Fijian culture. English should be encouraged as the medium of instruction, for it will have the advantage of keeping the young people in the English-speaking world, and of providing a common language which is not a component of those of the two hostile groups. Sports, in which all should be encouraged to take part will form an important part of extracurricular activities.

Fijians, Indians, and Europeans now meet in games and sports, in football Fijians preferring rugby and Indians soccer; cricket teams usually include members of all three races. Indeed, the greatest and most enthusiastic ethnic mingling in Fiji is in the field of sports. I watched a soccer game and also a field hockey game one afternoon in a tournament of the Department of Public Works: "Public Roads" against "Mechanics," "Carpenters" against "Head Office," and so on. Each team was made up of Fijians, Indians, and Europeans chosen according to their athletic ability. They tackled each other, jostled one another shoulder to shoulder, and passed the ball unselfishly to score goals. Perhaps it is no accident that the largest area of playing fields in the Colony is next to the great, imposing structure which is Government Headquarters. The British love of sports is reflected in Fiji. Boys of today and girls too playing together without regard to race, creed, or color will one day govern Fiji under a captain chosen by them all, obeying the same rules and regulations. It is sometimes said in Great Britain and Northern Ireland that the battle of Waterloo was won by discipline and leadership inculcated on the playing fields of Eton. The ethnic struggle in Fiji will finally be resolved on the sports area in Suva.

Post-script

Since the manuscript of this book was finished, a conference lasting two weeks in late July and early August, 1965, to discuss Fiji's constitutional future was held in London in response to an invitation from Britain. It was attended by the Governor of Fiji and the 18 unofficial members of the Legislative Council—six Fijians, six Indians, and six Europeans. It was stated in Fiji that the conference was "not the result of any general demand" of the representatives of the Colony or of the people. The British Secretary of State for the Colonies maintained that its purpose "was to work out a constitutional framework which would preserve a continuing link with Britain, within which further progress could be made in the direction of internal self-government" (15).

At meetings of sections of the population of Fiji which preceeded the conference, it was emphasized especially by Fijians that it would not deal with any aspect of independence or effort "to attenuate let alone abandon" the historical and happy association of Fiji with the United Kingdom. Indians, however, hoped that the Conference would "forge and mold a new constitution" which would ultimately lead to "complete independence in the not too distant future" (15).

Apart from the opening sessions of the Conference, the discussions were held in private, daily communique's indicating in general terms their subject matter. When the meetings were over it was reported that the rock on which the representatives split was whether elections in the Colony should be held on the basis of a common role for all the people, or whether the voting would be carried out on the basis of a communal role, that is a restricted number of candidates chosen to represent the major ethnic groups in the Colony.

It was proposed that a new constitution would provide for 36 elected members; nine Fijians, nine Indians, and seven Europeans would be elected on communal roles; two Fijians by the Council of Chiefs; and three Fijians, three Indians, and three Europeans on a cross-voting system in which voters of all the ethnic groups would take part. This proposal was accepted by the Fijian, European, and British delegations, but was opposed by members of the Indian delegation. They pressed for full internal self-government immediately, with elections on the basis of a straight common roll. They expressed "bitter disappointment" at the result of the conference (15).

As a result of the Conference in London, the Legislative Council, then existing, was dissolved in early August, 1966, and writs were issued for the election of a new Legislative Council which was voted into office at the end of the following September and the beginning of October. Because the islands are scattered over thousands of square miles, it took two weeks to record all the ballots. The people voted on the "racial and interracial basis" decided on, and, as was expected, the Europeans remained holding the balance of power between Fijians and Indians. The British Colonial Governor retains his traditional veto, but in the future mainly in matters of foreign relations and defense. From members of the new legislature, an Executive Council or Cabinet of six elected members took office together with four officers appointed by the Governor; they will exercise the executive powers of government. The new legislature was elected for five years.

Leading up to the election, the main Indian political

organization, the Federation Party, led by an ambitious lawyer, expounded the classic anti-colonial "one-man one-vote, undiluted democracy and no racialism," knowing that acceptance of that policy would, paradoxically, eventually bring Indian domination.

The Federation's main rival, the Alliance, was directed by a Fijian Chief of much charm and prestige. It was a loose coalition of political organizations embracing all races, including some anti-Federation Indians. Its platform supported the retention of "racial" representation in the Legislative Council. The election results showed strong support for Alliance candidates in Fijian and General constituencies and a clean sweep of Indian communal seats by the Federation Party.

As for independence, one prominent Fijian shrugged his shoulders to express a representative native view: "I guess we'll have to have it some day, but we want to take our time about it" (30).

APPENDIX 1

Longer Tables

TABLE 17

THATCH ROOFS AND IRON ROOFS (20, 51)

ETHNIC GROUP	*Number per 1,000 with roof of:*	
	THATCH	IRON
Fijian	633	361
Indian	406	589
European	16	949
Part-European	87	908
Chinese and Part-Chinese	31	967
Rotuman	554	443
Other Pacific Islanders	450	545
All Components of Population	474	520

TABLE 18
THE RELIGIONS OF FIJI
Proportion per 1,000 (20, 39)

ETHNIC GROUP	METHOD-IST	ROMAN CATH-OLIC	ALL CHRISTIAN DENOMI-NATIONS	HINDU	ISLAM	ALL NON-CHRISTIAN RELI-GIONS
Fijian	857	117	999	—	—	—
Indian	11	10	26	810	150	971
European	80	176	962	—	—	3
Part-European	439	434	991	—	—	—
Chinese and Part-Chinese	190	259	505	1	1	150
Rotuman	660	332	1,000	—	—	—
Other Pacific Islanders	310	258	998	—	—	—
All Component Populations	400	80	515	397	73	478

TABLE 19
INDIAN HOUSEHOLDS IN FIJI
AND THEIR LANGUAGES (20, 52)

LANGUAGE	NO. OF HOUSEHOLDS
Hindustani	17,164
Hindi	3,644
Tamil	1,498
Urdu	1,223
Gujerati	830
Telegu	797
Gurmukhi	468
Malayalam	134
All other	90
Not stated	183
TOTAL	26,031

TABLE 20

PROPORTION PER 1,000 INDIAN POPULATION
OF EACH SEX IN FIJI, 1956 (20, 34)

	Born in Fiji		Born in India and Pakistan	
AGE GROUP	MALE	FEMALE	MALE	FEMALE
0– 4	997	998	2	2
5–14	990	994	9	6
15–29	969	977	30	21
30–44	920	942	76	55
45–59	648	736	342	256
60–74	105	197	889	797
75 and over	33	58	960	933

TABLE 21

EXPORTS OF SUGAR FROM FIJI (11; 15; 30)

YEAR	TONS OF SUGAR	VALUE
1942	131,294	£1,761,055
1943	92,529	£1,345,286
1944	67,252	£1,035,616
1945	30,504*	£ 536,201
1946	106,473	£2,111,557
1947	112,433	£2,840,307
1948	149,494	£4,265,406
1960	219,109	no data
1962	200,402	£8,481,524

* The low return of 1945 was due to labor troubles.

TABLE 22

CULTIVATION OF SUGAR CANE BY ETHNIC
GROUP (20, 48)

RACE	PROPRIETARY MANAGERIAL AND EXECUTIVE	SUPERVISORY AND CLERICAL	OTHER WORKERS
Indian	8,791	45	8,047
Fijian*	479	5	782
Part-European	6	—	8
European	4	1	—
Chinese and Part-Chinese	4	—	—
Rotuman	—	—	2
All Other	4	—	6
TOTAL	9,288	51	8,845

* Excluding Fijians living in their villages.

TABLE 23

ACREAGES UNDER CROPS BY ETHNIC
GROUP, 1958 (16, 35)

CROP	TOTAL ACREAGE	INDIAN	FIJIAN	EUROPEAN AND PART-EUROPEAN	CHINESE AND OTHERS
Sugar cane	128,863	118,184	8,448	2,231	—
Rice	31,200	30,150	400	250	400
Coconuts	168,000	5,000	84,000	76,000	3,000
Bananas	5,000	380	4,600	20	—
Roots (Food)	35,933	2,877	31,696	—	1,360
All other[1] crops	9,997	3,672	4,860	210	1,300
TOTALS	378,993	160,218	134,004	78,711	6,060
Farming Population[2] Approximately		23,000	28,000	600	950

[1] Vegetables, fruit, cocoa, pulses, tobacco, etc.
[2] People, fifteen years and over.

In addition to the above, it is estimated that there are some 36,000 acres of improved pasture land, and 600 acres of fodder crops, mainly utilized by European dairy farmers.

TABLE 24

DISTRIBUTION OF LAND OWNERSHIP (16, 19)

FORM OF OWNER- SHIP	POPULA- TION IN 1965	PER CENT OF POP.	AREA OF LAND OWNED IN ACRES	PER CENT OF TOTAL AREA OF COLONY	REMARKS
1. Crown Land					
Freehold			85,424	1.9	
Schedule A[1]			120,000	2.6	
Schedule B[2]			88,000	1.9	
2. Freehold					
a. Colonial Sugar Re- fining Co.			75,091	1.7	Major portion leased to sugar cane farmers, mostly Indians
b. Europeans and Part- Europeans	14,212	4	246,242	5.5	
c. Indians	169,403	49	75,830	1.7	
d. Chinese	4,155	1.2	5,081	0.1	
e. Bananas			16,950	0.4	
f. Ellice Islanders	5,320	1.5	4,600	0.1	
g. Fijians	—	—	7,532	0.2	Registered titles
h. Other Races	91	0.03	2,688	0.06	
3. Native Customary Tenure					
a. Fijians	148,134	43	3,776,000	83.6	
b. Rotumans	4,422	1.3	11,000	0.24	
TOTALS	345,737	100.0	4,514,438	100.00	

[1] Schedule A lands are those which have reverted to the crown as *ultimus haeres* by virtue of the extinction of the owning *mataquali*. Rents derived from these lands are paid into general revenue.

[2] Schedule B lands are those for which no claims were made to the Native Lands Commission set up in 1880; rents from them are paid into a special fund controlled by the Fijian Affairs Board (16, 19).

TABLE 25
INCREASE IN INDIAN AND FIJIAN POPULATION
SINCE 1881 (16, 10)

YEAR	INDIAN	PER CENT OF TOTAL	FIJIAN	PER CENT OF TOTAL
1881	588	0.46	114,748	90.01
1891	7,468	6.16	105,800	87.31
1901	17,105	14.20	94,397	78.60
1911	40,286	28.87	87,096	62.42
1921	60,634	38.56	84,475	53.71
1936	85,002	42.85	97,651	49.22
1946	120,063	46.24	117,488	45.25
1956	169,403	49.00	148,134	42.85
1961	206,819	50.41	171,248	41.74

TABLE 26
CATTLE AND PIGS IN FIJI (20, 55)

	VITI LEVU AND ADJACENT ISLANDS	VANUA LEVU AND ADJACENT ISLANDS	ALL OTHER ISLANDS[1]	TOTAL
Cows	35,218	7,626	1,271	44,115
Calves under one year	17,615	3,954	552	22,121
Bulls and Steers	13,961	2,686	535	17,182
Working bullocks	22,012	6,486	70	28,568
Cattle unspecified	—	1,000	—	1,000
Total cattle	88,806	21,752	2,428	112,986
Pigs	7,423	2,717	11,204	21,344

[1] Provinces of Kadavu, Lau, Lomaiviti, and Rotuma.

TABLE 27
IMPORTS OF FIJI, 1962, AND THEIR SOURCES[1]

COMMODITY[2] AND MAJOR SOURCES	QUANTITY	VALUE £	PER CENT OF TOTAL IMPORTS	PER CENT FROM MAJOR SOURCES
TOTAL IMPORTS	—	17,386,146*	100.0	
Food	—	3,643,581	20.9	
Flour	10,816 sh. tons	407,634	2.3	
Australia	10,698 ,, ,,	402,615		98.8
Sharps & Pollard	17,731 ,, ,,	642,306	3.7	
Australia	17,731 ,, ,,	642,306		100.0
Meats	3,095,501 lbs.	306,498	1.8	
New Zealand	2,790,603 ,,	266,602		87.0
Fish	3,316,504 ,,	252,500	1.5	
Un. So. Africa	2,440,750 ,,	152,467		60.4
Beverages & Tobacco		444,825	2.6	
Crude Materials, inedible, except fuels	—	328,964	1.9	
Timber	5,092,012 sup. ft.	260,728	1.5	
Canada	4,715,057 ,, ,,	234,491		89.9
Mineral fuels, lubricants, related minerals	—	2,239,161	12.9	
Motor Fuel	6,495,189 gal.	388,593	2.2	

Indonesia	4,273,556 ,,	257,892		66.4
Diesel oil	51,355 tons	625,938	3.6	64.0
Indonesia	31,687 ,,	400,870		
Animal and Vegetable oils and fats	—	225,433	1.3	
Chemicals	—	1,285,770	7.4	
Fertilizers	15,608 ,,	291,002	1.7	
Japan	14,952 ,,	274,229		94.2
Manufactured goods				
Classified by material	4,472,463 sq. yd.	3,898,369	22.4	
Cotton Fabrics	2,258,025 ,, ,,	427,789	2.4	44.4
India	338 ,, ,,	189,843		
Silk Fabrics	148 ,, ,,	248	—	
United Kingdom	17 ,, ,,	63		25.4
Japan		15		6.0
Jute bags & sacks	7,347 cwt.	53,128	0.3	94.6
India	6,966 ,,	50,265		
Machinery & Transport equipment		3,512,865	20.2	
Machinery & Electrical Appliances		2,433,413	14.0	55.6
United Kingdom		1,353,068		
Motor Cars & Trucks	956 nos.	730,349	4.2	59.7
United Kingdom	582 nos.	435,748		

TABLE 28

PRINCIPAL EXPORTS OF FIJI, 1962, AND THEIR DESTINATIONS[1]

COMMODITY[2] AND MAJOR DESTINATIONS	QUANTITY	VALUE £	PER CENT OF TOTAL EXPORT	PER CENT MAJOR DESTINATIONS
TOTAL EXPORTS (DOMESTIC)		12,492,790*		
Food		9,077,264	72.7	
Sugar, raw	200,402 tons	8,481,524	67.9	
United Kingdom	100,628 ,,	5,162,413	1.4	60.9
Bananas, fresh	151,772 72-lb. case	175,131		
New Zealand	149,775 ,,	172,318	0.2	98.4
Beverages & Tobacco		24,020		
Crude materials, inedible, except fuels	6,862 tons	682,781	5.5	
Copra		389,314	3.1	
Miscellaneous Manufactured articles		1,550,629	8.9	
Miscellaneous Transactions and Commodities		256,549	1.5	

[1] Statistics received from Fiji, January 24, 1964.
[2] According to the Standard International Trade Classification.
* Total includes gold: £3,593.

	Quantity	Value	%	%
Japan	6,862 "	389,314		100.0
Mineral fuels, lubricant, related materials	—	—	—	—
Animal and Vegetable oils and fats			11.6	
Coconut oil	18,188 tons	1,452,991	11.6	
United Kingdom	6,640 "	1,452,918		37.5
		544,793	0.1	
Chemicals	—	10,566	0.1	
Manufactured goods classified by material	—	13,116	—	
Machinery & Transport Equipment	—	2,109	9 5	
Miscellaneous Transactions and Commodities	—	1,190,987	0.3	
Miscellaneous Manufactured Articles	—	38,956		

[1] Statistics received from Fiji, January 24, 1964.
[2] According to the Standard International Trade Classification.
* Total includes gold: 84,926 fine oz. £1,189,011.

TABLE 29
BIRTH RATE PER THOUSAND (45, 225)

YEAR	EUROPEAN	EURONESIAN	FIJIAN	INDIAN
1954	17.14	36.91	37.00	43.17
1955	15.76	30.29	34.17	42.26
1956	14.59	33.21	35.69	44.47
1957	22.63	29.86	38.69	44.73
1958	22.03	33.60	35.40	44.52

TABLE 30
DEATH RATE PER THOUSAND (45, 225)

1954	4.02	4.39	11.00	8.60
1955	3.19	4.15	9.61	7.18
1956	4.05	4.64	7.52	7.19
1957	5.63	4.85	8.54	6.29
1958	4.90	5.20	7.56	6.54

TABLE 31
PER CENT OF POPULATION INCREASE (16, 7; 15)

CENSUS OF	TOTAL POPULATION	% INCREASE FROM LAST CENSUS	AVERAGE ANNUAL % INCREASE SINCE 1901
1901	120,124	—	—
1911	139,541	16.16	1.50
1921	157,266	12.70	1.19
1936	198,379	26.14	1.56
1946	259,638	30.88	2.74
1956	345,737	33.16	2.91
1958	374,284	8.25	3.71
1961	413,872	10.57	4.00
1962*	427,850	3.17	4.17

* Estimated

APPENDIX 2

Glossary of Fijian Words (65)

buli, Fijian official who is head of a *tikina.*

galala, free, at liberty; exempt (as from duty or tax).

kerekere, a system of acquiring things by begging for them from a member of one's own group.

koro, a village.

lala, the order of a chief requiring work to be done.

levu, big, great, large (Viti Levu, Great Fiji).

levuka, the middle of a thing.

loma, the inside of a thing; *loma-ni-koro,* the interior of a village.

mataquali, the primary social division in Fiji, larger than *i tokatoka,* and smaller than *yavusa.*

meke, a native dance.

niu sigani, copra.

ratu, title of rank or respect before the name of a chief.

rewa, high; Rewa River.

roko, roko tui, a title of honor for the official in charge of a province, as Roko Tui Bau.

sulu, a loin cloth, skirt; piece of cloth two yards long girt around the loins.

suva, a mound, heap of earth, serving as a land mark.

taukei, i, the owner or possessor of a thing; the land owners.

taveuni, the source of supply of a country.

tikina, a subdivision of a province.

tokatoka, i, the enlarged family unit or group; a unit of Fijian society.

turaga, a chief, head man; *turaga-i-taukei,* head of a *vanua, turaga-ni-koro,* head of a village.

vaka, like, according to; *vaka-Viti,* in the Fijian fashion.

vanua, land, region, place; *Vanua Levu,* large region.

Viti, Fiji, the general name in the west of the islands; in the east the Tongan pronunciation, Fiji, is used.

yau, goods, wealth, possessions.

yavusa, the largest kinship and social division of Fijian society.

Fijian Plants (47; 65)

bahonga, a fern, *Polypodium sp.*

balawa, see *varawa.*

boka, see *dalo.*

buco, buco tabua, breadfruit, *Artocarpus incisa, Urticaceae;* also, *uto.*

cassava, (Eng.) tapioca, *Manihot sp.*

coboi, lemon grass, *Andropagon coloratus.*

dakua, dakua makadre, Dammaria vitiensis, Coniferae.

dalo, the taro plant, much used as a food; *boka,* in some islands; vars. *Caladium esculentum, Aroidae; Colocasia antiquorum.*

daunini, yam; vars. *Dioscorea alata; vurai, Dioscorea nummularia; tikau* wild yam.

kava, see *yaqona.*

kumala, the sweet potato, *Babatas edulis, Convolvulaceae.*

niu, coconut, *Cocos nucifera, Palmaceae.*

pateta, (Eng.) potato, *Solanum tuberosum.*

tikau, see *daunini.*

uto, see *buco.*

vakeke, hibiscus, *Hibiscus abelmoschus.*

varawa, balawa, pandanus; *Pandanus verus, Pandanaceae; Angiosperma monocotyledoneae.*

vurai, see *daunini.*

vutu, a tree, *Barringtonia edulis.*

yabia-dina, Tacca pinnatifida, Taccaceae; erroneously called "arrow-root."

yaqona, kava in Polynesia, *Piper methysticum.*

Indian Names and Words

achar, a condiment used to flavor food; probably a local folk term.

Arya Samajis, a modern Hindu organization that seeks to persuade Hindus to return to the Vedas.

bara, an Indian dish; probably a local folk term.

Bhagwat, see *Srimal Bhagwat Katha.*

Bihar, a state in northern India.

Brahma, in Hindu religion the highest and assolute divinity, the supreme spirit, the primary creator; first member of the Hindu Triad.

Brahman, Brahmin, a member of the highest caste among Hindus.

coriander, an apiaceous plant, *Coriandrum sativum,* used in cookery by the Indians.

dahl, varieties of pulses, lentils.

dhoty, a loin cloth worn by men in India.

Dravidian, pertaining to linguistic groups of southern India.

ghee, rendered butter; butter clarified by boiling.

Gujerat, a state in western India.

Gurmuki, a Sikh dialect.

Hindi, an Aryan language of northern India.

Hindustani, a *lingua franca* related to Hindi spoken in what was British India.

Holi, a generic term for a festival something like the Mardi Gras in New Orleans.

Jagriti, name of a Hindu newspaper in Fiji.

Jullunder, a district in Punjab state in India.

Katha, see *Srimal Bhagwat Katha.*

Kisan sangh, kisan, peasant, *sangh,* association; name of a labor union in Fiji.

Ludhiana, a district in Punjab state.

Maha Sangh, maha, great, *sangh,* association; name of a labor union in Fiji.

Madras, a state in southern British India.

Malayalam, one of the Dravidian languages of southern India.

Mariamman, folk term for a female goddess.

Muslim, Moslem; a follower of Mohammed.

Nepal, an independent state north of India.

panchayat, a council of men who settle disputes. It may apply to a caste or a village.

Puja, worship of an image of any deity.

puri, puffed bread fried in deep *ghee.*

Ram, a Hindu god; *Rama,* an incarnation of Vishnu, one of the Hindu Triad.

Ramlila, the epic story of the Hindu deity Rama.

roti, bread made from flour.

Sanatan Dharmis, a sect of Hindus.

sehna, a vegetable dish; probably a local folk term.

Sikh, a member of a religious sect of northern India.

Srima Bhagwat Katha, a Hindu semi-religious festival based on Vedic literature.

Sunni, a large division of Muslims.

Tamil, one of the Dravidian languages.

Telugu, one of the Dravidian languages.

Urdu, a dialect of Hindi written in Arabic script.

Uttar Pradesh, a state in northern India.

Vishnu, one of the Hindu Triad.

Zebu, humped cattle, *Bos indicus,* widely domesticated in India and other countries.

AUTHOR'S NOTE: Some of the words—of Hindu, Muslim or Sikh origin—are from folk versions of traditions of India. Cora Du Bois, Zemurray Professor of Anthropology at Harvard University, helped me with some of the meanings. She read the chapters on the Indians, and made suggestions which I followed up.

APPENDIX 3

Selected References on the Pacific Islands by the Author
(arranged chronologically)

Population and Utilization of Land and Sea in Hawaii, 1853. Bernice P. Bishop Museum Bulletin 88, 1931, pp. 1–33.

"Manoa Valley, Honolulu: A Study in Economic and Social Geography." Bull. Geog. Soc. Phila, Vol. 30, No. 4, pp. 109–130. 1932. (Alfred Gomes Serrao co-author).

"The Island of Hawaii." Journ. Geog., Vol. 31, No. 6, Sept. 1932, pp. 225–236.

"The Oahu Sugar Cane Plantation, Waipahu." Econ. Geo. Vol. 9, No. 1, Jan. 1933, pp. 60–71.

"Land Utilization in the Hawaiian Islands." University of Hawaii Research Publications, No. 8, 1933, pp. 1–140.

"Pineapple Industry in Hawaii." Econ. Geog. Vol. 10, No. 3, July 1934, pp. 288–296.

A Gazetteer of the Territory of Hawaii. University of Hawaii Research Publications, No. 11, 1935, pp. 1–241.

"Hawaiian Toponymy." In *A Gazetteer of the Territory of Hawaii.* University of Hawaii Research Publications, No. 11, 1935, pp. 231–239.

"Small Farming on Kauai, Hawaiian Islands." Econ. Geog. Vol. 12, No. 4, Oct. 1935, pp. 401–409.

Chinese Rice Farmers in Hawaii. University of Hawaii Research Publications, No. 16, 1937, pp. 1–72. Chee Kwon Chun, co-author.

"The Territory of Hawaii." In *The American Empire,* (Haas, ed.), pp. 216–305. University of Chicago Press, 1940.

"Land Utilization in American Samoa." Bernice P. Bishop Museum, Bulletin 170, 1941, pp. 1–48.

"Changes in Land Utilization in South Sea Islands." The Scientific Monthly, Vol. 55, July, 1942, pp. 60–65.

Fiji: Little India of the Pacific. University of Chicago Press, 1942, pp. 1–176.

"Impact of the War on South Sea Islands." Geog. Rev., Vol. 36, No. 3, July 1946, pp. 409–419.

"Environment, Race and Government in South Sea Islands." Scott. Geog. Mag., Vol. 63, No. 2, 1947, pp. 49–56.

"The United States' Trust Territory of the Pacific Islands." Journ. Geog. Vol. 47, No. 7, Oct. 1948, pp. 253–267.

Geography of the Pacific, O. W. Freeman, ed. Chapter 7, "Eastern Melanesia," pp. 173–204. John Wiley and Sons Inc., 1951.

"Potential Resources and Prospects of Future Development of Non-Selfgoverning Territories in the Pacific." Proc. Seventh Pacific Science Congress, Vol. 7, 1953, pp. 508–523.

The Pacific Dependencies of the United States. The Macmillan Company, New York, 1957, pp. 1–388.

"Great Britain in Hawaii: The Captain Cook Monument," The Geographical Journal, Vol. 130, Part 2, June 1964, pp. 256–261.

"The Economy of New Caledonia," Tokyo Geographical Society, Journal of Geography, Vol. 73, No. 6, 1964, pp. 321–336.

"Man and the Ecosystem," Cahiers de Géographie de Quebec, Institut de Géographie, Université Laval, No. 19, Oct. 1965–March 1966, pp. 355–358.

References

1. Belshaw, C. S.; "Indian Peasants in Fiji," *Economic Development and Cultural Change,* Vol. 11, No. 3, Part 1, April 1963, pp. 333–334.
2. Bezar, George; "Tourism: Fiji's New Million-pound Industry," *South Pacific Bulletin,* July, 1960, pp. 36–37, 74.
3. Brewster, A. B.; *Hill Tribes of Fiji.* London, 1922.
4. Burns, Sir Alan; *Fiji.* London, 1963.
5. Cato, A. C.; "Fijians and Fiji-Indians, A Culture-Contact Problem in the South Pacific," *Oceania,* Vol. 26, 1955–1956, pp. 14–34.
6. Chapman, Brian; "A Review of the British Political Elite by W. L. Guttsman." *Manchester Guardian Weekly,* Aug. 22, 1963, p. 10.
7. Colony of Fiji, "Central Archives of Fiji and Western Pacific High Commission." Certain correspondence of his Excellency the Acting Governor of Fiji (Sir Charles Major) to the Secretary of State for the Colonies. Telegram dated 6th April, 1909. Dispatch dated 19th April, 1909. Photostat copy in library of J. W. Coulter.
8. ———; "Central Archives of Fiji and Western Pacific High Commission." Committee on Emigration from India to the Crown Colonies and Protectorates. Part II, Fiji, 1909. Photostat copy in library of J. W. Coulter.

9. ———; "Central Archives of Fiji and Western Pacific High Commission." Public (Emigration) Dispatch to India. No. 39, dated 24th March, 1875. Photostat copy in library of J. W. Coulter.

10. ———; "Commissioners Annual Reports for the Year 1957." Legislative Council of Fiji, Council Paper No. 40 of 1958. Suva.

11. ———; "Fiji Information." Public Relations Office, Suva. Published quarterly. Various numbers.

12. ———; "Fiji: Handbook of the Colony." Suva, 1937.

13. ———; "Geological Survey Department, Annual Report for the Year 1958." Legislative Council of Fiji, Council Paper No. 17 of 1959.

14. ———; "Lands, Mines and Surveys, Annual Report for the Year 1958." Legislative Council of Fiji. Council Paper No. 19 of 1959.

15. ———; "News From Fiji." Public Relations Office, Suva. Various numbers.

16. ———; "Report of the Commission of Enquiry into the Natural Resources and Population Trends of the Colony of Fiji, 1959." Legislative Council of Fiji, Council Paper No. 1 of 1960. (Commonly referred to as "The Burns' Report.")

17. ———; "Report of the Council of Chiefs, 1959." Legislative Council of Fiji, Council Paper No. 29 of 1959.

18. ———; "Report of the Fiji Sugar Enquiry Commission." Legislative Council of Fiji, Council Paper No. 20 of 1961.

19. ———; "Report of the Sugar Board of Enquiry, 1959." Legislative Council of Fiji, Council Paper No. 26 of 1959.

20. ———; "Report on the Census of the Population, 1956." Legislative Council of Fiji, Council Paper No. 1 of 1958. (20 a. 1946.)

21. ———; "Report on Fiji for 1957." Colonial Office, London, 1958.

22. Coulter, J. W.; Field notes on United Provinces (Uttar Pradesh) and other parts of Northern India.

23. ———; Field notes taken during three visits to Fiji.

24. ———; *Fiji: Little India of the Pacific.* University of Chicago Press, 1942, pp. 1–156.

25. Deane, W.; *Fijian Society or the Sociology and Psychology of the Fijians*. London, 1921.

26. Deed of Cession of Fiji to Queen Victoria of the United Kingdom of Great Britain and Ireland. Appendix A in Burns' *Fiji*, pp. 233–236.

27. Derrick, R. A.; *The Fiji Islands: A Geographical Handbook*, Suva, 1951.

28. Dutt, R. P. *India Today and Tomorrow*. London, 1955.

29. Fairchild, H. N.; *The Noble Savage: A Study in Romantic Naturalism*. New York, 1928.

30. *Fiji Times*, Suva. Various editions.

31. Gabel, N. E.; *A Racial Study of the Fijians*. University of California Press, 1958.

32. Gangulee, N. N.; *Problems of Rural India*. Calcutta, 1928.

33. Green, F. C.; "Rousseau and the Idea of Progress." *The Zaharoff Lecture for 1950*. Oxford, Clarendon Press, 1950.

34. Henderson, G. C.; *Fiji and the Fijians, 1835–1856*. Australia, 1931.

35. Hooker, E. R.; *Readjustment of Agricultural Tenure in Ireland*. University of North Carolina Press, 1938.

36. Hopcraft, Arthur; "Where a Tin Roof is a Sign of Wealth." *Manchester Guardian Weekly*, Vol. 89, No. 23. Dec. 5, 1963.

37. Im Thurn, E. F.; *Thoughts, Talks and Tramps, A Collection of Papers*. No. 12, "A Study of Primitive Character." London, 1934.

38. Joyce, T. A.; *Customs of the World*. London, 1912–13, Vol. 1, pp. 101–111.

39. Mayer, Adrian C.; *Peasants in the Pacific; A Study of Fijian Indian Rural Society*. University of California Press, 1961.

40. McMillan, A. W.; *The Indians in Fiji*. Suva, 1944.

41. Memorandum for Sir Alan Burns G.C.M.G., Chairman, and Members of the Commission of Inquiry. Presented by The Five Indian Members of the Legislative Council and Other Signatories on behalf of the Indian Community of Fiji. Suva, 4th July, 1959. Library of J. W. Coulter, p. 42, mimeographed.

42. Morison, T.; *The Economic Transition in India*. London, 1911.

43. Mukhtyar, G. C.; *Life and Labour in a South Gujarat Village.* New York, 1930.

44. Neale, W. C.; *Economic Change in Rural India: Land Tenure and Reform in Uttar Pradesh* (i.e., The United Provinces), 1800–1955. Yale University Press, 1962.

45. *Pacific Islands Year Book,* Eighth Edition. R. W. Robson, ed. Sydney, 1959.

46. *Pacific Review.* Suva. Editorials, July 21 and July 28, 1960.

47. Parham, B.E.V.; *Fijian Plants.* Fiji Society of Science and Industry, 1938–1939, Suva.

48. Parham, H.B.R.; *Fiji Plants.* Supplement to Journal of the Polynesian Society, Memoir No. 16. Polynesian Society, Wellington, 1943.

49. Pomfret, J. E.; *The Struggle for Land in Ireland, 1800–1923.* Princeton University Press, 1930.

50. Robson, R. W.; *A Close Look at Vital Sugar Report.* Pacific Islands Monthly, Vol. 32, No. 3, pp. 57–60.

51. Roth, G. K.; *Fijian Way of Life.* Oxford University Press, 1953.

52. Roth, G. K.; "Native Administration in Fiji During the Past 75 Years: A Successful Experiment in Indirect Rule." Royal Anthropological Institute, Occasional Paper No. 10. London, 1951.

53. Sanders, R. T.; "Interlude," in Burns' *Fiji,* pp. 149–173.

54. Sarkar, Jadunath; *Economics of British India.* Calcutta, 1911.

55. Spate, O.H.K.; *The Fijian People: Economic Problems and Prospects.* Legislative Council of Fiji. Council Paper No. 13 of 1959.

56. (The) *Statesman's Year Book,* 1961–1962. S. H. Steinberg, ed.

57. Thompson, Basil; *The Fijians: A Study of the Decay of Custom.* London, 1908.

58. Usher, L. G.; "Analysis of Three Races in Fiji," *Pacific Islands Year Book,* Eighth Edition, pp. 278–280, 1959.

59. Vaughan, C. E., (ed.); *The Political Writings of Jean Jacques Rousseau.* Vol. 1, New York, 1962.

60. *Village Life in Northern India: Studies in a Delhi Village.* University of Illinois Press, Urbana, 1958.

61. Wallace, F. C.; *Culture and Personality,* New York, 1961.

62. Webb, M. de P., *India's Plight.* London, 1934.

63. Whitney, B. B., (ed.); *Six Cultures. Studies of Child Rearing.* The Rajputs of Khalapur, India, by J. T. Hitchcock and Leigh Minturn, pp. 207–361. New York, 1963.

64. Williams, Thomas; "Fiji and the Fijians," Vol. 1, *The Islands and their Inhabitants.* London, 1858.

65. Capell, A.; *A New Fijian Dictionary.* Sydney, 1941.

66. Gillion, K. L.; *Fiji's Indian Migrants, A History to the End of Indenture in 1920.* Melbourne, 1962.

67. Silsoe, Lord; *Report of the Fiji Coconut Industry Survey.* Colony of Fiji, Suva 1963.

Index

Items in the index are grouped under eight headings: Agriculture, Forests, Gazetteer, Government, Land, Population, Social and Religious Factors, and General.

221

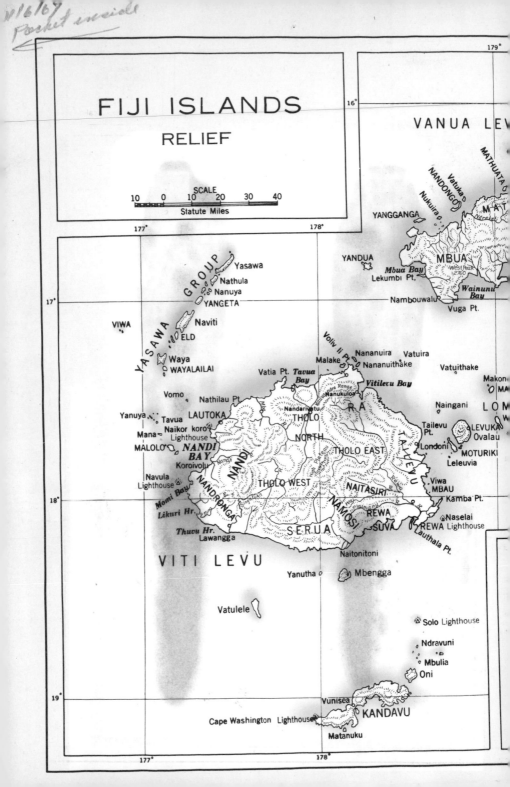

W16/67
Pocket inside

FIJI ISLANDS
RELIEF

SCALE
10 0 10 20 30 40
Statute Miles

177°   178°   179°

16°

VANUA LEV

MATHUATA

NANDONGO
Vatuka
Nukuira
MAT

YANGGANGA

YANDUA
Mbua Bay
Lekumbi Pt.
MBUA
West Peak
2760
Wainunu
Bay

Nambouwalu
Vuga Pt.

17°

YASAWA GROUP
Yasawa
Nathula
Nanuya
YANGETA

VIWA
Naviti
ELD
Waya
WAYALAILAI

Voliv II Pt.
Malake
Nananuira   Vatuira
Nananuithake
Vatuithake
Makon
MA

Vatia Pt. Tavua Bay
Vitilevu Bay

Vomo
Nathilau Pt
Oro Range
Nanukuloa
RA
Naingani
LOM

Yanuya
Tavua   LAUTOKA
Mana
Naikor koro
Lighthouse
MALOLO
NANDI BAY
Koroivolu
Nandarivatu
THOLO
NORTH
THOLO EAST
Tailevu Pt.
Londoni
LEVUKA
Ovalau
MOTURIKI
Leleuvia

Navula
Lighthouse
NANDRONGA
Momi Bay
Likuri Hr.
Thuvu Hr.
Lawangga
NANDI
THOLO WEST
NAITASIRI
NAMOSI
REWA
SERUA   SUVA
Viwa
MBAU
Kamba Pt.
Naselai
REWA Lighthouse
Lauthala Pt.

18°

VITI LEVU
Naitonitoni
Yanutha   Mbengga

Vatulele

Solo Lighthouse

Ndravuni
Mbulia
Oni

19°

Vunisea
Cape Washington Lighthouse
KANDAVU
Matanuku

177°   178°